The
FRIENDSHIP
BOOK

of Francis Gay

A THOUGHT
FOR EACH DAY
IN 2006

D. C. THOMSON & CO., LTD.
London Glasgow Manchester Dundee

Grant me the quiet charm which friendship gives,
Which lives unchanged, and cheers me while it lives.

John R. Newell

January

A ND he said, The Lord is my rock, and my
fortress, and my deliverer. The God of
my rock; in him will I trust: he is my shield,
and the horn of my salvation, my high tower, and
my refuge, my saviour; thou savest me from
violence.

Samuel II 22:2-3

C LOSE your eyes and picture
A place within your mind,
A green and tranquil garden
Where trouble's left behind.
Imagine, too, the sunlight
That warms the peaceful air,
And dances on the blossoms
That graceful branches bear.
Now pause awhile and listen
To birdsong, soft and sweet,
Breathe in the scent of flowers
That bloom around your feet.
Just use imagination,
And you may find it's true
A little glimpse of heaven
Is just within your view.

Margaret Ingall.

TUESDAY — JANUARY 3.

IT'S that time of year when we call to mind a dozen new months. Here's a good recipe for them:

Prepare one day at a time, and into each put 12 parts of faith, 11 of patience, 10 of courage, 9 of work, 8 of hope, 7 of fidelity, 6 of open-mindedness, 5 of kindness, 4 of rest, 3 of prayer, 2 of meditation, and 1 of well-selected resolution.

My cookery book tells me: *add a teaspoonful of good spirits, a dash of fun, a pinch of folly, a sprinkling of play and a heaped cupful of good humour.*

Next, pour love generously into the whole, cook thoroughly, garnish with a few smiles and a sprig of joy; then serve with quietness, unselfishness, and cheerfulness.

Now, isn't that a good recipe for a new year?

WEDNESDAY — JANUARY 4.

JOHN HARRIS, the Cornish poet, was one of a family of ten. He started work at the age of nine and four years later was toiling in the depths of a mine.

Despite his lack of education he loved poetry and wrote constantly using whatever means he could. Indeed, some of his verses were penned in blackberry juice because he had no ink. In twenty years as a miner he produced sixteen volumes of poems.

A stained glass window at Troon, in Cornwall, commemorates John Harris, who died in 1884, a man who triumphed over adversity.

SERENITY

THURSDAY — JANUARY 5.

HAVE you climbed any mountains recently? Yes, I agree, not many of us could nod our heads in answer to that question! But what I'm talking about are not rocky peaks but the metaphorical mountains we sometimes encounter — the challenges which seem so daunting that no sensible person would even attempt them.

But my friend Ron is a mountain climber. When the children in his village needed a playground, he ignored all the gloomy voices that scoffed at the idea of ever raising enough money.

Instead he set about organising all kinds of fund-raising events, rallying friends, and cajoling local businesses into supporting the scheme. Amazingly, within just one year the playground had turned from a distant dream into a reality.

As one of his doubters later admitted, "You really taught me a lesson. Next time I'll remember the adage — those who say something can't be done, shouldn't interrupt those who are doing it!"

FRIDAY — JANUARY 6.

EVERY snowflake is different. We probably think they are exactly the same, but in fact they couldn't be more dissimilar.

Isn't it often the same with ourselves? We generalise so easily, talk about groups of people doing one thing or another, forgetting that all of us are individuals, with unique thoughts, dreams and desires.

Next time you're out on a busy street do remember that.

SATURDAY — JANUARY 7.

THE Border collie is well known for rounding up sheep — other dogs (to their owners' shame) might chase birds. Well, in the United States, the Border collie is actually trained to do just that!

Birds have always been a danger to aircraft on airport runways and in Florida, because egrets, sandhill cranes and others are protected species, any attempts by airport staff to disperse them safely were unsuccessful.

Jet, a Border collie, began a special training programme called Bird Strike to chase these birds and South-West Florida International Airport at Fort Myers agreed to give him a trial. In 1999 a successful Jet was the first-ever bird dog employee and proved to be amazingly efficient at his work, which was carried on later by his successor, Radar.

More Border collies are being trained for this specialist work in the United States, not only at airports, but also on golf courses, at corporate office parks and even fish farms which suffer from waterfowl feeding from heavily-stocked ponds!

A particularly good example of man's best friend working with us in perfect harmony.

SUNDAY — JANUARY 8.

AND God made two great lights: the greater light to rule the day, and the lesser light to rule the night: he made the stars also.

Genesis 1:16

MONDAY — JANUARY 9.

WHETHER I'm busy or just pottering in the garden, I often enjoy a few minutes of what I call "over the fence garden chat" with our neighbour, John.

He was away in Australia one New Year, but he sent a cheerful card wishing both myself and the Lady of the House health and happiness in the months to come. It was a card which was just a little different, for John had added the following words:

"I wish you also the thoughts that savor of content, the quiet mind is richer than a crown."

To have such thoughts is a blessing indeed, and I'd like to pass on these sentiments to you all today.

The words quoted were written by the Elizabethan man of letters, Robert Greene.

TUESDAY — JANUARY 10.

ONE of the best thoughts on failure which I have come across is this one, printed in a church magazine:

"Don't fear failure so much that you refuse to try new things. The saddest summary of a life contains three descriptions — could have, might have and should have."

WEDNESDAY — JANUARY 11.

HERE is a good "Rule To Live By", passed on by a Yorkshire correspondent.

"The tongue weighs practically nothing, but so few people can hold it."

PULLING HER WEIGHT

THURSDAY — JANUARY 12.

CLOCKS have a lot to teach us. They keep us right about the time, of course, but they do much more.

Their steady tick tells us not to rush things but to do them at an even pace. Their faces have a serenity and a stillness that soothes and — the most important lesson of all — their hands never go backwards.

A reminder that we, too, must keep moving forward with confidence in what lies ahead.

FRIDAY — JANUARY 13.

ALONG LIFE'S WAY

IN life there's body language,
That can see us through each day.
It speaks as if advising
In a very special way.

Put your best foot forward
On whatever route you take,
And try to keep a level head
On decisions you may make.

Give pessimists the elbow
If they try to catch your ear.
Make no bones about it —
A helping hand brings cheer.

Whatever cares we shoulder,
It seems prudent to recall
This kind of body language
Can be helpful to us all.

John M. Robertson.

SATURDAY — JANUARY 14.

JANET, who had just celebrated her ninety-second birthday, shared this life-enhancing recipe with us:

"Look on age," she said, "as being like a bumper bank account of happiness, growing with the days and weeks, the months and years.

"Call it your Bank of Memories. Pop in and deposit an instalment of brightness each day.

"Keep up your deposits. By adding steadily to your account, you will soon have lots of goodness to withdraw from and, as a bonus, the interest will cheer the passing years."

Thank you, Janet, for that piece of priceless advice.

SUNDAY — JANUARY 15.

BUT the Lord is the true God, he is the living God, and an everlasting king.

Jeremiah 10:10

MONDAY — JANUARY 16.

A WISE teacher I knew used to tell her pupils to take some "nourishing time" in the middle of her lectures.

"We must all know when to stick to the task and when to take a break," she said. "There is always a time to persist and a time to take respite."

Good thinking, don't you agree? Enjoying a breather doesn't mean you are abandoning the task in hand — and you'll begin again with greater enthusiasm.

TUESDAY — JANUARY 17.

I WONDER if you know these words written about compassion by Geoffrey Chaucer, creator of the vivid and colourful "Canterbury Tales":

"Humblest of heart, highest of reverence, benign flower, crown of virtues."

Beautiful 14th-century words, which are as true now as when they were written. Today, as yesterday, there is never too much compassion in the world; so many are in distress and suffering, and are in need of sympathy and help.

WEDNESDAY — JANUARY 18.

L OCK this up within your heart,
Neither lose nor lend it:
Two it takes to start a quarrel,
One can always end it.

THURSDAY — JANUARY 19.

I WOULD like to pass on to you today these words from the writer and thinker Celia Luce:

"A small trouble is like a pebble. Hold it too close to your eye, and it fills the whole world and puts everything out of focus.

"Hold it at a proper distance, and it can be examined and properly classified.

"Throw it at your feet, and it can be seen in its true setting, just one more tiny bump on the pathway of life."

A useful thought to remember when life is challenging.

FRIDAY — JANUARY 20.

THESE wise, if somewhat blunt, lines were written by a friend in my autograph book years ago. A warning: you have to read them slowly!

He that knows not and knows not that he knows not is a fool — shun him.

He that knows not and knows that he knows not is teachable — teach him.

He that knows and knows not that he knows is asleep — awaken him.

He that knows and knows that he knows is wise — follow him.

SATURDAY — JANUARY 21.

EACH of us, I'm sure, has a special memory of someone's wonderful smile. Most memorable smiles shine through in a moment of true happiness, but in contrast a friend once chose a moment of sadness for his favourite recollection.

"Times of joy and gladness always generate a smile," he said, "but I have also found that the most beautiful smiles in the world are the ones that struggle through the tears.

"It's as if they have been called on to bring some light to a darkened day. A case of smiling through the clouds of the moment."

SUNDAY — JANUARY 22.

IT was planted in a good soil by great waters, that it might bring forth branches, and that it might bear fruit, that it might be a goodly vine.

Ezekiel 17:8

MONDAY — JANUARY 23.

SAYING grace before a meal is an admirable custom, but why stop there? Thomas Lamb, the English writer, favoured giving thanks before setting out on a walk, before meeting friends, reading a book and other simple pleasures.

We have so many things to be grateful for; pausing now and again to say thanks is surely the least we can do.

TUESDAY — JANUARY 24.

HERE is a thought to cheer you today: you may be only one person in the world, but you may also be all the world to one person.

WEDNESDAY — JANUARY 25.

OUR friend Sheila returned from a round-the-world trip taken to celebrate her retirement.

"Just look at these!" she said, showing us an album of attractive colour photographs. "I want to share with you my memories of these wonderful places which I was fortunate enough to visit. Just look at this shot of the Taj Mahal. Oh, and aren't the Canadian Rockies magnificent?"

There were other striking views, too, such as Sydney Harbour by night, and the Golden Gate Bridge in San Francisco.

How good it is to be fascinated by what we see on our travels, whether on a simple half-hour drive to a favourite spot near home, or a long flight to a far-away city. Life is not measured by the number of breaths we take, but by the great moments which take our breath away.

THURSDAY — JANUARY 26.

I WISH you Summer memories
To warm each Winter's day,
And all the hope and joy of Spring
When Winter slips away.
I wish you many blessings
Along the path you tread,
And all the love of all the years
To light the way ahead.

Iris Hesselden.

FRIDAY — JANUARY 27.

MOST of us, at some point, feel stressed as we tackle a new and difficult task.

At times like these, as we inch towards our goal, I have often found it useful to keep in mind this proverb:

"The gem cannot be polished without friction, nor can man be perfected without trials."

SATURDAY — JANUARY 28.

JEAN took her four-year-old grandson Mark to a family-friendly restaurant. On the way out, after their meal, he was presented with a big red balloon attached to a string, and he played with it happily all the way back to where the car was parked.

Then, before climbing inside, he suddenly let go of the string and watched the balloon disappear upwards.

"Why did you let it go?" asked Jean.

"I gave it to God to play with," came the instant reply.

SUNDAY — JANUARY 29.

THINE, O Lord, is the greatness, and the power, and the glory, and the victory, and the majesty: for all that is in the heaven and in the earth is thine; thine is the kingdom, O Lord, and thou art exalted as head above all.

Chronicles I 29:11

MONDAY — JANUARY 30.

THE Ford Motor Company, started in 1903 by Henry Ford, owed much of its success in mass production to teamwork, a quality in which every worker and manager was a believer.

Let me share with you today these words from Mr Ford himself: "Coming together is a beginning, staying together is progress, and working together is success."

Teamwork is the real name of every successful game, both on and off the field.

TUESDAY — JANUARY 31.

WHEN it comes to good, sound common-sense, you can't beat my angling friend Bert. He is the most patient man I know, an attitude learned from his many years waiting and watching for a catch.

"It's just like life," he says. "You can't expect to pull out a big fish right away. Anyway," he adds, "the longer you wait the more you appreciate your luck when it comes — and the better the fish will taste!"

Yes, Bert has learned a few lessons along the riverbank.

ICE HOUSE

February

DO you know these lines? I came across them one day, and I thought I would share them with you:

Over the Winter glaciers I see the Winter glow,
And through the wild piled snowdrift,
The warm rosebuds below.

Rich in optimism, I find these lines very appealing, a beautiful combination, written by the philosopher and poet Ralph Waldo Emerson.

PRAYER FOR A JOURNEY

DEAR Lord, as I go travelling
Be with me, on my way,
And please, if I grow weary,
Then strengthen me, I pray.
And if my footsteps falter,
Please keep me on the track,
And if I lose direction
Please guide me safely back.
And when the time approaches
For me to cease to roam,
Please take my hand in yours, Lord,
And lead me safely home.

Margaret Ingall.

FRIDAY — FEBRUARY 3.

WHEN the Lady of the House returned from a sewing group meeting she was smiling. "While we were stitching," she explained, "our old friend Mary happened to start humming 'My Favourite Things' which led to the rest of us discussing just what we'd add to our own personal list.

"Laura chose the smell of freshly-cut grass, Jo wanted the sight of kites flying on a windy day. Sue decided on lapping waves, and I chose firelight on a Winter's evening. But it wasn't until later that we realised every single thing we had chosen was free. It just goes to prove," she finished triumphantly, "that money may buy some good things, but it certainly doesn't buy the best."

Now that's wisdom beyond price!

SATURDAY — FEBRUARY 4.

AS the wife of the President of the United States, Eleanor Roosevelt was known, loved and respected not merely for her position, but for the wise and caring person that she was.

Never content with words alone, she actually put good intentions into practice, running a factory for the jobless, setting up and teaching at a school for poor children, and being an ardent advocate of equal rights for all. "I have never felt that anything really mattered but the satisfaction of knowing that you stood for the things in which you believed, and had done the very best you could," she once said.

A woman worthy of the title First Lady.

SUNDAY— FEBRUARY 5.

SO the last shall be first, and the first last: for many be called, but few chosen.

Matthew 20:16

MONDAY — FEBRUARY 6.

TO me there is something very special about twilight. Whether it's Winter, when the frosty blue sky and bright moon remind us that it's time to close the curtains and light the fire, or Summer, when the warm afternoons deepen slowly into soft and fragrant dusk, I still find it a special moment.

It's a time to halt awhile, to let go the busy cares of the day, and simply enjoy the beauty of the world around us.

TUESDAY — FEBRUARY 7.

A FOURTEEN-YEAR-OLD girl once went for a swim in the Solway Firth off the Scottish coast. Caught in a current she was almost drowning when she prayed that, if spared, she would devote her life to the service of others. At once her feet touched rocks and she struggled to safety.

When she grew up she was chosen as bride by Prince Henry, later Duke of Gloucester, and threw herself into her duties. The Red Cross, the St John Ambulance Brigade, and the forerunner of Meals On Wheels were only three of the charities she supported.

During her life of over 100 years, Princess Alice fulfilled the promise she had made as a young girl.

DEEP ROOTS

WEDNESDAY — FEBRUARY 8.

THERE are times when even a clergyman can feel a little downhearted.

Dr Robert W. Dale of Birmingham was a renowned preacher a century ago at the prestigious Carrs Lane Church. For some reason he was under a dark cloud one day when a woman he barely knew came up to him and exclaimed: "God bless you, Dr Dale. If you could only know how blessed you have made me feel hundreds of times!"

Then off she went, little realising that she had given him a much-needed tonic.

In his journal Dr Dale commented: "At that moment, the mist broke, the sunlight returned, and I again breathed the free air of the mountains of God."

THURSDAY — FEBRUARY 9.

I SUSPECT we've all done this — put something away in a "safe place", only to find out later that it was a little too safe. This happened to our friend, Suzanne, who used the time it took hunting for the lost item to make up a verse about her predicament:

I put it in a safe place, of that I'm very sure,
I knew it was important to keep it quite secure,
So why, now that I'm searching in every
little nook,
Do I know I'll never find it until the last place
that I look?

Fortunately, Suzanne has never yet misplaced her sense of humour!

FRIDAY — FEBRUARY 10.

"I WISH you enough . . ." a visitor said one evening as he left.

"May I ask what that means?" I enquired, rather curious.

Peter smiled. "Yes, it's a genuine wish that has been handed down from other generations. My parents used to use it regularly.

"When they said 'I wish you enough', they were wanting the other person to have a life filled with just enough for a good and satisfying life."

Here are the words of this wish:

I wish you enough sun to keep your attitude bright. I wish you enough rain to appreciate the sun more. I wish you enough happiness to keep your spirit alive.

I wish you enough pain so that the smallest joys in life appear much bigger. I wish you enough gain to satisfy your wanting. I wish you enough loss to appreciate all that you possess. I wish you enough hellos to get you through the final goodbye.

SATURDAY — FEBRUARY 11.

CHINESE proverbs are admired and repeated all over the world for their blend of poetic language and ancient wisdom. This one, although not typical, particularly appeals to me and was sent to me by an overseas reader:

"To attract good fortune, go out and spend a new coin today on an old friend, share an old pleasure with a new friend, and lift up the heart of a true friend by writing his name on the wings of a dragon."

CATWALK

SUNDAY — FEBRUARY 12.

NOW these are the commandments, the statutes, and the judgments, which the Lord your God commanded to teach you, that ye might do them in the land whither ye go to possess it.

Deuteronomy 6:1

MONDAY — FEBRUARY 13.

WHEN reading the reminiscences of Mary Soames, daughter of Winston Churchill, I could not but be impressed by her stories of the wisdom she picked up from her famous parents. Here is a good example:

"My father taught me never to let the sun go down on my wrath. I learned never to be ashamed of saying that you are sorry — have no false pride about it, even to young children."

TUESDAY — FEBRUARY 14.

*D*O not go, unquestioning,
   Wherever the path may lead,
Go, instead, where there is no path
   And others will take heed.
Do not follow the straight road,
   The one which has no bends,
Strike out instead across the hills
   To where the rainbow ends.
Do not follow the old route
   Afraid that you might fail,
Go, instead, where there is no path
   And leave behind a trail!

Iris Hesselden.

WEDNESDAY — FEBRUARY 15.

THORA Hird was a much-loved personality, not only for her considerable talent as an actress, but also for her Christian approach to life, her humour and down-to-earth wisdom. Although the demands of her career meant she had to leave her native Lancashire, she managed to find happiness wherever she lived.

"Neighbours," she once wrote, "are just the funny mixed bag of people with whom you happen to share a street, a block of flats, a mews or a village.

"You get to know one another and become friends because you know, for better or worse, you're all in the same boat, and life will be better for everyone if you all pull together. And if that means you having to put up with their funny ways, remember, they're also putting up with yours."

Now that's the kind of neighbour we'd all like next door!

THURSDAY — FEBRUARY 16.

I'VE been reminded how Charles Kingsley, the poet and novelist, approached the arrival of each new day. "Thank God when you get up each morning," he said, "that you have something to do this day which must be done.

"Doing your best in the small tasks will breed in you temperance and self-control and a thousand virtues which the idle never know."

Let us now think of everyone who deserves credit for doing the smaller, but vital, things.

FRIDAY— FEBRUARY 17.

I'VE always known Geoff to be a keen walker, but even I was surprised to learn he was planning to undertake a sponsored trek from John O'Groats to Lands End.

"I was inspired," he told me, "by a quote from Horace Walpole. He said that human beings 'are often capable of greater things than they perform. They are sent into the world with bills of credit, and seldom draw them to their full extent'. So I've decided to start cashing mine in."

It's a novel way of putting it, but I do like that idea. Next time I feel my reserves are running low, I'll think of those bills of credit, and remember I may be richer than I think!

SATURDAY — FEBRUARY 18.

LORNA had been looking forward to a day's shopping expedition when her neighbour tripped and broke an ankle. Suddenly, instead of choosing new clothes Lorna found herself babysitting her neighbour's seven-year old son.

"And do you know," she told me later, "I was amazed to find how quickly I got over my disappointment. I thought the day would drag, but by the time we'd made a get-well card and a big batch of peppermint creams for his mother, it was time for him to go home."

We can't always be in control of life, but we can do our very best to be in charge of our attitude to it. Lorna's cheerful approach certainly made her day sweeter than it might otherwise have been!

SUNDAY — FEBRUARY 19.

THERE is none holy as the Lord: for there is none beside thee: neither is there any rock like our God.

Samuel I 2:2

MONDAY — FEBRUARY 20.

JOHN WESLEY, the great preacher and founder of Methodism, very nearly lost his life at the age of six when the family home in Epworth, Lincolnshire, went on fire on a dark Winter's night.

Two men spotted the little boy at a window and pulled him from the blaze just before the roof fell in.

No wonder he always described himself as "a brand plucked from the burning".

And what a "brand" he proved to be!

TUESDAY — FEBRUARY 21.

OUT of the cold and frozen earth
The tiny shoots appear,
And always take me by surprise
At this time of year.
These dainty, fragile drops of white
On slender stalks of green,
Have somehow sprung up overnight
Upon the Winter scene.
They are the first of all the flowers
To brave the ice and cold —
Who gives the secret strength they have
To stand there brave and bold?

Kathleen Gillum.

CLIMB EVERY MOUNTAIN

WEDNESDAY — FEBRUARY 22.

I ONCE came across the following on a poster in a library: "Words are silver, but silence is gold."

The aim was to remind those seeking knowledge in the vast reading-room that it is good to use words in speech, but equally worthwhile to repeat them to yourself in silence, digesting them fully. I'd never suggest that we cut down on our daily conversation, but saying little at times is often a wise choice.

Abraham Lincoln put it humorously when he said: "It is better to be silent and be thought a fool than to speak out and remove all doubts!"

Diodicus, the fifth-century philosopher said: "A properly-kept silence is a beautiful thing — it is nothing less than the father of very wise thoughts."

THURSDAY — FEBRUARY 23.

"TODAY would have been Uncle Jim's birthday," said Josie, glancing at the calendar. "Even after all these years, I never forget. He was such a wonderful receiver of presents.

"Whatever gift we children had planned," she explained, "he accepted it with the greatest enthusiasm. Whether it was home-made biscuits, a photo-frame or a knitted scarf, he was always pleased. It meant, of course, that we enjoyed his birthdays as much as he did."

Uncle Jim sounds as if he was the sort of person we'd all like to know. After all, to show pleasure in receiving is your gift to the giver!

FRIDAY — FEBRUARY 24.

OUR friend Jack was telling me about the time during his student days when a professor asked some of his students to answer questions in a quiz. The last question was: "What is the first name of the woman who cleans the entrance hall?"

John wasn't the only student who wondered if this might be some kind of a joke. He voiced his thoughts.

"Nothing of the kind," the professor told him, assuring everyone that the question would count in the final score.

"In your careers," he said, "you will meet many people. Remember that all of them are significant. They each deserve your attention and care, even if all you do is smile and say 'hello'."

Today Jack confesses that he has never forgotten that quiz question, or the lesson it taught him. Always take an interest in the people you meet and work with.

SATURDAY — FEBRUARY 25.

A FEW friends were talking one afternoon about growing older, and how some people like to keep their age a secret, when our friend Linda quipped:

"My mother will have to stop making herself out to be younger than she is, because soon I'm going to be older than her!"

Here's an oft-repeated thought that is apt in this context: "It's not the years in your life that count. It's the life in your years."

SUNDAY — FEBRUARY 26.

BE thou exalted, O God, above the heavens: let thy glory be above all the earth.

Psalms 57:11

MONDAY — FEBRUARY 27.

HOW often do we laugh? Apparently six-year-olds laugh about three hundred times a day, but adults are said to average a mere forty-seven times, and some considerably less than that.

A stress consultant was so concerned about this that he opened a "Laughter Clinic" to which customers flocked. Some health professionals and employers are being trained to introduce life-enriching laughter into the workplace.

Laughter is a great stress reliever, and Sir Harry Secombe was a great practitioner of it. "Laughter," he once said, "is cathartic. It can lift the heart and is a good base for marriage, and indeed for any relationship."

It's fun, it has no side effects, and it doesn't cost anything. Can you find something to laugh at now? And someone to laugh with?

TUESDAY — FEBRUARY 28.

THE Scottish social reformer, surgeon, and writer Samuel Smiles wrote these words in the 19th century:

"Self-respect is the noblest garment with which a man may clothe himself, the most elevating feeling with which the mind can be inspired".

An excellent thought for today, so let's keep it in mind!

March

SPRINGTIME

THERE'S a banner of green in the
hedgerow now,
There's a flicker of Spring in the air;
There's a chatter of birds in the tree-top bough,
And the earth's waking up everywhere!
There's a smile in the sky, as a puffball cloud
Sails by on its platter of blue —
There's a promise of hope, in the green
shoots proud,
And there's Spring, in the first morning dew.

Elizabeth Gozney.

"REGRETS . . . I've had a few," runs the song, but are such negative-sounding thoughts to be encouraged?

Katherine Mansfield, the writer, certainly made her feelings clear on the subject when she said:

"I have made it a rule through the years never to feel regret and never to look back. Regret is an appalling waste of energy. You can never build on regret. It is only good for wallowing in."

It's only common sense to learn from our mistakes, but when we have, it's time to move on.

FRIDAY — MARCH 3.

JIM, who runs a successful business, says he owes much to this tip from one of the world's greatest soldiers.

It came from General George S. Patton, who once said: "Never tell people how to do things. Tell them *what* to do and they will surprise you with their ingenuity."

Jim finds that every person, from the newest recruit to the most senior employee, responds to that style of management. An attitude worth adopting, I'm sure, in many walks of life.

SATURDAY — MARCH 4.

I WONDER if you are familiar with that lovely old hymn, "Just As I Am"? It was written by Charlotte Elliott who, born in 1789, grew into a pretty and talented young woman. Sadly, however, by her thirties her health began to fail, leaving her feeling dispirited.

It was then she met the evangelist, Dr Caesar Malan, who encouraged her to seek help through Jesus, and to come to Him "just as you are".

Inspired by those words, Charlotte Elliott not only became a devout Christian, but used her skills to write her famous hymn — one which was not only instrumental in helping her brother raise money for a charity school, but which even now continues to touch hearts and minds:

Just as I am, without one plea,
But that Thy blood was shed for me,
And that Thou bidd'st me come to Thee,
O Lamb of God, I come!

SUNDAY — MARCH 5.

THOU, O Lord, remainest for ever; thy throne from generation to generation.

Lamentations 5:19

MONDAY — MARCH 6.

MUCH as I admire the quality of bravery, I'm always rather bemused when folk start talking about it as if it's some kind of possession that only a few of us are lucky enough to be given.

Courage is always to be admired, but surely bravery is not some external gift, rather the inner acknowledgement of fear and a deliberate determination to overcome it. One of the best descriptions I ever heard came from Dorothy Bernard, who said, "Courage is fear that has said its prayers."

Next time you're feeling a little daunted about anything, try putting that into practice.

TUESDAY — MARCH 7.

AS a boy in the 1790s Charles Waterton spent all his time in the woods and fields around his home at Walton, near Wakefield, Yorkshire. He loved watching the birds and animals and when he was older went searching for specimens in the wilds of South America, writing a book about his adventures.

Back home he created at Walton what is believed was the world's first nature reserve. Another first was the nestboxes he attached to trees in the park.

We've much to thank Charles for.

WEDNESDAY — MARCH 8.

I MET my philosophical friend, Howard, early one day as I took a morning walk.

"You look pensive," I remarked. "Which thoughts cross your mind on this lovely morning?"

"We're enjoying a spell of great weather at the moment," he replied, "and it inspires two thoughts. First, that every new day is a gift from God to us."

"And the second?" I asked.

"And the second is that what we do with it is our gift to God."

Howard always gives me something to think about.

THURSDAY — MARCH 9.

THE QUEST

*L*IFE'S an adventure, a journey, a quest,
  A seeking for knowledge and truth,
Discovering beauty and wonder and joy,
  Recapturing dreams of our youth.

Life is a gift and one made for sharing,
  A time to find laughter and tears,
A time of great changes, of mountains to climb
  And love growing strong through the years.

You may go exploring faraway lands,
  Or travel each day in your mind,
The quest is important, the journey worthwhile
  With still more adventures to find!

                                        Iris Hesselden.

BRAVING THE COLD

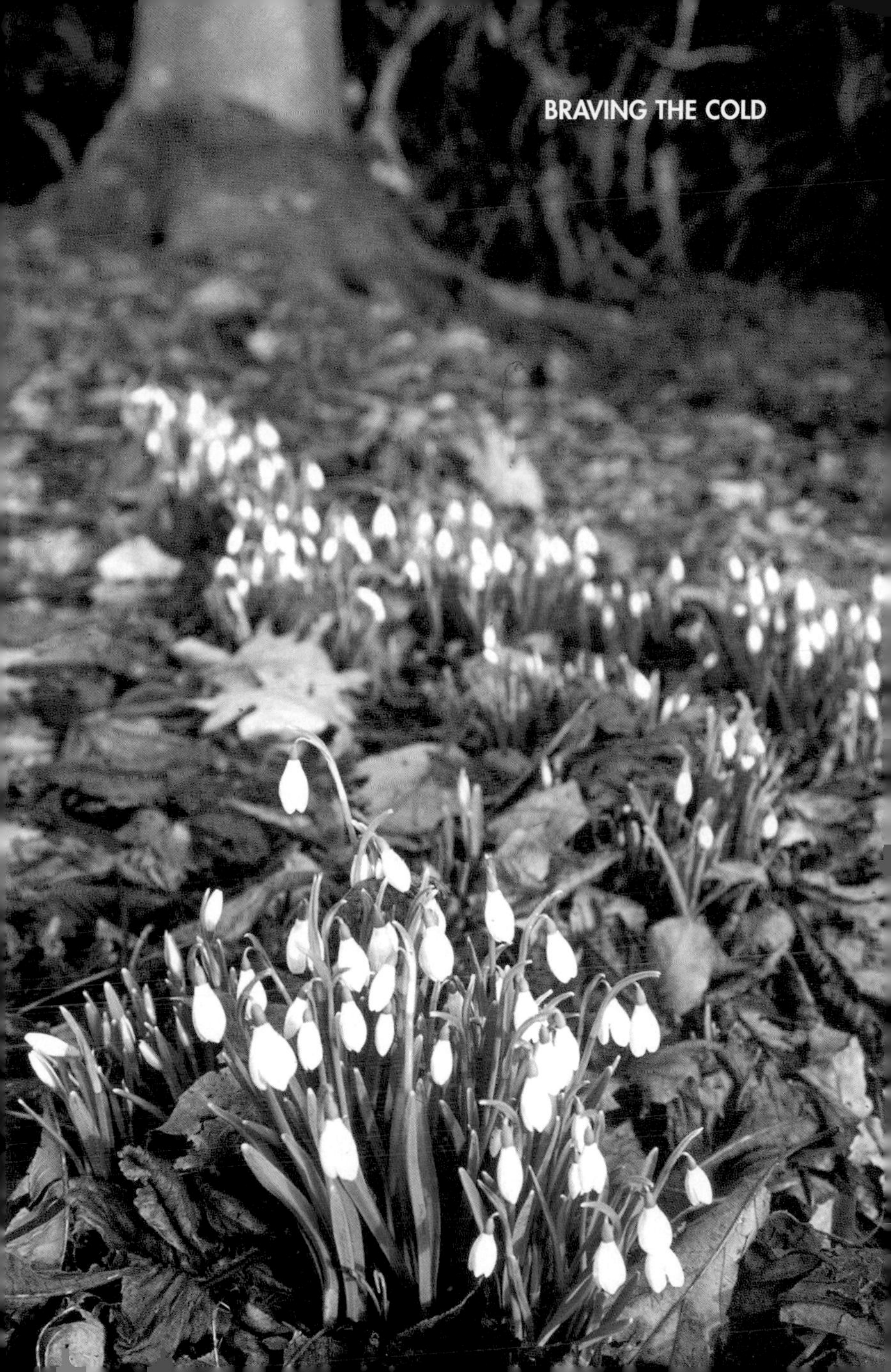

FRIDAY — MARCH 10.

THE Lady of the House and I decided to lay a new carpet in our much-used "book-room" — it is too small to call a library — and have both the walls and the numerous shelves painted. We were soon busy clearing furniture, books, magazines and Great-Aunt Louisa's much-loved diaries and scrapbooks.

A welcome break for tea and biscuits saw us sitting on a box of books dipping into one of the treasured diaries. One entry read:

March 10th. — Boisterous, blowy March with its mix of Spring and Winter, has seen Margaret and myself busy washing paintwork, blankets and curtains. Now, I rather like the Elizabethan name for Spring-cleaning — the sweetening! Oh, yes, and just this minute I have thought of a perfect collective name for folk like those I overheard talking so unpleasantly yesterday. They were undoubtedly "an unkindness of gossips". Such idle chat can cause a great deal of distress.

Now I must go and help Margaret hang the clean curtains in the drawing-room.

SATURDAY — MARCH 11.

WHEN our friend Murray passed on, many tributes were paid to him, particularly to his cheerful nature. Murray was always smiling and joking.

Now, I think the best tribute came from the man who said, "Murray must have been the only baby ever born not crying but laughing!"

What a lovely way to be remembered.

SUNDAY — MARCH 12.

AND there appeared an angel unto him from heaven, strengthening him.

Luke 22:43

MONDAY — MARCH 13.

THE ups and the downs of daily living bring us both pleasure and exasperation.

We sometimes talk of being in a Monday morning "down" mood, then another time we might say we are in an "upward-looking" frame of mind.

These expressions come together in a wise piece of advice once given by the Rev. Jesse Jackson, the American civil rights leader:

"Never look down on anybody unless you're helping them up."

Words worth remembering, I'm sure.

TUESDAY — MARCH 14.

CHRISTINE, a wise friend, said: "People rush into things too much. The world moves so fast that to be non-stop is fashionable. Why don't we go a little more slowly?"

It is exactly the advice that the great seventeenth-century French dramatist Molière gave when he said: "All you have to do is pause — it is our impatience that spoils things."

Molière, whose real name was Jean Baptiste Poquelin, adopted the virtue of patience as an actor and writer. "Have patience with all things, but chiefly have patience with yourself," he said.

Patience is indeed a virtue.

WEDNESDAY — MARCH 15.

A FRIEND, Helen, pinned up this verse in the senior citizens' club where she is an energetic and enthusiastic member who enjoys the great variety of activities there:

Now, what is the use of supposing
The dire things that could happen to you,
Or worry about some misfortune
That seldom, if ever, comes true?

If you really want to be happy
And get rid of the "misery of dread",
Just give up supposing the worst things
And look for the best things instead.

THURSDAY — MARCH 16.

A LTHOUGH writer C. S. Lewis was a renowned scholar and teacher, it is undoubtedly as author of the Narnia books that he remains best known. These remarkable Christian allegories written for youngsters, set in a land of myth and magic, have already entertained and inspired several generations of children.

However, it wasn't all plain sailing for the author. Not only was C. S. Lewis over fifty years old when he published the first in the series, it was also against the advice of many friends, who feared such a work might jeopardise his reputation as a serious writer.

Fortunately, he was not discouraged. "You are never too old to set another goal or to dream a new dream," he once wrote. Now, that's a piece of wisdom aimed at adults.

FRIDAY — MARCH 17.

WHEN James I of England instructed the leading scholars of the day to make a new translation of the Bible, they produced the version which we call the Authorised or King James' Bible.

Some say that one of the compilers was William Shakespeare who was then 46 years old and that he secretly wrote his name into Psalm 46. The forty-sixth word of the psalm is "shake" and the forty-sixth word from the end is "spear".

Whatever the truth of this, Psalm 46 is a great comfort and inspiration to many:

God is our refuge and strength: a very present help in trouble. Therefore we will not fear . . .

SATURDAY — MARCH 18.

"TIME may be a great healer," I once overheard someone say, "but it definitely isn't a very good beautician."

The observation certainly made me smile in rueful agreement, but I rather prefer the view of writer Martin Buxbaum. "Some people," he said, "no matter how old they get, never lose their beauty — they merely move it from their faces into their hearts."

Now that idea has an appeal which is more than just skin-deep!

SUNDAY — MARCH 19.

AND thou shalt go to thy fathers in peace; thou shalt be buried in a good old age.

Genesis 15:15

MONDAY — MARCH 20.

WHAT do you consider to be the best piece of advice you have ever been given?

The Lady of the House and I were discussing this question with a few friends one day. Isobel, who is a teacher, quoted these words which a former pupil had delivered in a prizegiving speech to final-year students.

It was the advice, she recalled, which Abraham Lincoln gave to a young man setting out on his career. "Whatever you are," said Lincoln, "make sure you are a good one."

TUESDAY — MARCH 21.

ONE of our friend Albert's local churches has a "Thought For The Day" notice board where anyone can add contributions. Here are some that have caught his attention:

"Try to see people's lamps, not their shades."

"Turn yourself into a window and bring light into someone's life."

"A smile is a curve which helps set things straight."

WEDNESDAY — MARCH 22.

BILLY has a medical condition which means he will never grow up, never do the things his brothers and sisters may do. But a happier boy I have never met and to his parents, Jim and Ada, he is a source of joy.

Ada once summed up their feelings for Billy in these simple words, "We love him for what he is and we love him for what he is not."

THURSDAY — MARCH 23.

ONE early Spring day I saw a neighbour, a keen gardener, planting out seedlings. "Isn't that a bit risky, Gordon?" I asked. "It's very early, still time for late frosts to kill them off."

Gordon had a ready answer. "Of course it's risky, Francis, but you have to take chances at times! I follow a good example: our Lord took risks when He chose simple fishermen to be His disciples, and when He rode into Jerusalem to face Pilate. How different the world would be if He had not!"

Indeed, and there's a good chance that Gordon's hardy seedlings will survive and reward him with a fine show of flowers.

FRIDAY — MARCH 24.

THE famous eighteenth-century economist Adam Smith suggested a sound approach to the problems we all encounter in the course of our lives. He said:

"There is nothing that can be added to the happiness of a man who is in health, out of debt, and has a clear conscience."

SATURDAY — MARCH 25.

THE English language is full of expressions relating to the sea. "Keep a sharp lookout" is one, while "a safe haven" is another.

Here is a proverb that was new to me and which you, too, may not have heard before: "If you harbour bitterness, happiness will dock elsewhere."

SUNDAY — MARCH 26.

FOR he is not a God of the dead, but of the living: for all live unto him.

Luke 20:38

MONDAY — MARCH 27.

PEOPLE may regret the passing of their youth and yet, if we listen to young people, they often have many preoccupations and concerns — fear of failure, lack of confidence, concern about the future and the thought, do I measure up to my friends in appearance and achievement? I think the things older citizens may admire most are enthusiasm, curiosity and energy.

As we grow older, we manage to overcome most of our youthful fears but if we can go forward with optimism and a sense of wonder and joy, our age will always be unimportant. We will keep within us the spirit of youth and that cannot be defeated by age!

TUESDAY — MARCH 28.

THREE thoughts on gratitude for us to consider today:

The person who has stopped being thankful has fallen asleep in life.

R. L. Stevenson.

Gratitude is heaven itself.

William Blake.

There is a calmness to a life lived in gratitude, a quiet joy.

Ralph H. Blum.

WEDNESDAY — MARCH 29.

JUST one step can start a journey,
Just one step is all it takes,
Just one match can set a lantern
Burning bright till morning breaks.
Just one voice can launch an anthem,
Start a song that never ends,
Just one smile can bridge a silence,
Turning strangers into friends.
Just one deed of simple trusting
Sometimes very hard can seem,
Don't despair, for just one footstep,
Leads the way to find your dream.

Margaret Ingall.

THURSDAY — MARCH 30.

HERE is a quote for those among us who may be worried. It comes from the well-known lady of song, Lena Horne, who once said:

"It is not the load that breaks you down. It's the way you carry it."

There is no burden that can't be eased by adjusting the way we tackle its weight.

FRIDAY — MARCH 31.

SAMUEL PEPYS whose famous diary gave not only a vivid picture of his times, but also a revelation of his character, penned these words:

"Mighty proud am I and ought to be grateful to God Almighty that I am able to have a spare bed for my friends."

Friendship — a gift as old as the God-given hills, isn't it?

April

BUSY MINUTES

I'VE got all kinds of hobbies
I practise every day,
I fill the busy minutes
In every kind of way.
I like to be creative,
To knit and sew and bake,
There's nothing I won't tackle,
No item I won't make,
And though my eager efforts
Don't constantly come right
There's one thing I make daily
Before I sleep at night,
I make the time for stillness,
To pause awhile and say
How glad I am for all the joy
My hobbies bring each day.

Margaret Ingall.

AND Jesus, when he was baptized, went up straightway out of the water: and, lo, the heavens were opened unto him, and he saw the Spirit of God descending like a dove, and lighting upon him.

Matthew 3:16

MONDAY — APRIL 3.

LOVE can make us gentle, patient, caring, humble, appreciative, considerate, understanding, generous and kind.

Love is what keeps us from being hateful, unkind, envious, boastful, proud, vain and rude. It helps us not to insist on having our own way all the time, and it helps us not to be irritable, resentful or malicious.

Words to consider today and every day.

TUESDAY — APRIL 4.

WHEN things go wrong, and her spirits are low, our friend Sadie always thinks of these simple words from an American proverb:

"The soul would have no rainbow if the eyes had no tears."

WEDNESDAY — APRIL 5.

IT'S that season again, time to think about Spring-cleaning, and to throw out clutter from our homes — and the workplace!

We often find that, once we have cleaned out desks or other storage spaces, we have cleared space in our minds as well. Clutter is often linked to stress and procrastination, so if you feel overwhelmed by daily tasks, why not try a little Spring-cleaning, whatever the time of year?

I like what the well-known actor Robin Williams said: "Spring is Nature's way of saying, 'Let's party'!"

Why not celebrate the coming of a new season and start afresh at home and at work?

THURSDAY — APRIL 6.

IT was a cold Spring morning, but Reg felt it was an appropriate time to dig his garden. He hadn't been working very long when he paused to wipe sweat off his face and remarked to a neighbour who was standing nearby: "My word, it's getting warm! We'll have the Summer upon us soon at this rate!"

A few moments later, the spectating neighbour began to shiver, and as he buttoned up his jacket he commented: "Well, it feels cold to me. No sign of Summer yet surely!"

Isn't it remarkable how often two different people can respond to the same situation in very different ways?

FRIDAY — APRIL 7.

FOR more than twenty-five years the pianist Albert Semprini broadcast his "Semprini Serenade", a joyful mixture of music of all kinds. He introduced each programme with the same gently spoken words," Old ones, new ones, loved ones, neglected ones . . ."

He practised hard, treating each piece with respect, giving the time and patience to play it well, whether it was a demanding classical composition, a piece of light music or an arrangement of a popular song. Not surprisingly, Semprini gained a large and devoted audience.

Our friends and acquaintances are not unlike Semprini's music. They need our time and patience — the old ones, the new ones, the loved ones and the neglected ones.

SATURDAY — APRIL 8.

HERE is a story which you'll enjoy. We have in our safe keeping a pretty Victorian love brooch; made of silver, it bears the name "Sarah".

When her widowed father re-married, Sarah was unsettled at home, and left to work in an ironmonger's shop. Quite a step for a young clergyman's daughter in the 1800s! One day George, who had a contractor's business, came into the shop, and as one member of the family put it: "that was that" — it was love at first sight.

Sarah's brooch which George gave her is embellished with small trails of ivy for fidelity, tiny forget-me-nots for love and remembrance, and three-leafed clovers for good luck.

Of course, George and Sarah experienced both good and not-so-good times together, but their marriage was a long and happy one, blessed with children.

Sometimes Victorian brooches carried the word *Mizpah* — "may the Lord watch between me and thee, while we are absent one from another". A wish which, today as yesterday, expresses all our thoughts of a loved one, when they are apart from us.

SUNDAY — APRIL 9.

AND they worshipped him, and returned to Jerusalem with great joy: and were continually in the temple, praising and blessing God. Amen.

Luke 24:52-53

WATER FEATURE

MONDAY — APRIL 10.

EVERYBODY loves the ladybird, that pretty little creature that turns up most years in the garden. Now, did you know that it used to be called "Our Lady's Bird"? Its red colour was seen as resembling the cloak worn by the Virgin Mary in old paintings.

Count its spots and you will find there are seven and they were believed to be a reminder of seven joys and seven sorrows in Mary's life.

So the humble ladybird holds a special place in religious lore.

TUESDAY — APRIL 11.

A FRIEND read these words on the wall in a busy city office:

Everybody has the right to be upset, but that does not give us the right to upset those around us!

WEDNESDAY — APRIL 12.

THE Lady of the House was looking thoughtful as she arranged daffodils in a vase. "Don't you think," she mused, "that there's something very special about this time of year?"

I knew exactly what she meant, for at Eastertide I, too, am always moved to step back from day-to-day life, to pause and ponder on matters far bigger than this world. Perhaps the religious leader and writer Douglas Horton expressed it best when he said, "On Easter Day the veil between time and eternity thins to gossamer."

Now that is putting it at its best and most beautiful.

THURSDAY — APRIL 13.

THERE is still a lot of good in the world, as Berlin's daily newspaper, the "Berliner Morgenpost", showed when it appeared in an edition containing almost nothing but good news.

The editor said that bad news would not completely disappear that day but would be confined to small boxes on each page. For one day, readers were able to discover what a positive-spirited city they lived in. From the sports news to features all the contents were upbeat.

This newspaper, which normally had 32 pages, was expanded to 48 to contain all the cheerful reports! The idea for this special edition came from the newspaper staff themselves, who felt there was so much to praise in their city.

Now, isn't this a commendable idea? Let's keep looking for the good news and the good things in our lives — and not just for one day only. There is a lot of it around, if we take time to find it.

FRIDAY — APRIL 14.

A PARADOX, according to my dictionary, is a "seemingly self-contradictory statement" — and here are three that I particularly like:

"Nothing is so strong as gentleness; nothing so gentle as real strength." St Francis de Sales.

"Shared joy is double joy: shared sorrow is half sorrow." Swedish proverb.

"The more you give away, the richer you become." Anon.

SATURDAY — APRIL 15.

HERE'S a lovely thought for Easter — "Thou art the sun of other days, they shine by giving back thy rays."

Those words come from John Keble's "The Christian Year". He was a 19th-century cleric, theologian, poet and writer of hymns. Memorable words for us to keep in mind today.

SUNDAY — APRIL 16.

HE is not here, but is risen: remember how he spake unto you when he was yet in Galilee.

Luke 24:6

MONDAY — APRIL 17.

THIS is the month when thousands flock to Tombstone in Arizona to see and admire its roses. The Rose Tree Museum, housing the world's largest rose tree, draws the crowds.

The original rose bush was planted in the year 1885 by a young Scottish bride, Mrs Henry Gee, after her family had shipped her a box of shrubs from home. In it were a few rooted shoots of the Lady Banksia Rose. Now grown to over 8,000 square feet, it develops thousands of white blossoms, an enthralling sight when April comes round.

Isn't it good to know that these wonderful white blossoms in the Arizona town of the legendary O.K. Corral will be blooming again this April, as fine a symbol of love and friendship as the roses that are famously red in favourite poems and sayings?

TUESDAY — APRIL 18.

"**D**O you like my new umbrella?" asked Maureen, as I met her in the street one wet afternoon. "It was a gift from my neighbour, Pat."

I had to agree that it was a remarkably cheerful-looking affair of buttercup-yellow material patterned with a profusion of bright daisies and other flowers.

"Pat knows how much I hate the rain," continued Maureen. "But nowadays I find myself quite looking forward to grey skies, in case they give me the chance to show off my lovely present."

Isn't it amazing how a little generosity can bring sunshine to the cloudiest day!

WEDNESDAY — APRIL 19.

A LITTLE KINDNESS

S OMEONE listens, someone shares,
Someone hears and someone cares,
Someone says a kindly word
And joy and hope are gently stirred.

Someone is in need of you,
Needs a cheerful line or two,
Be the one to light their day,
Sending happiness their way.

Someone needs a friendly smile,
Just to make their day worthwhile,
Show a little kindness too,
And kindness will return to you.

Iris Hesselden.

THURSDAY — APRIL 20.

EVERY great man or woman has to start off somewhere. Read about the lives of notable people and you will often find they showed diligence and determination from an early age.

I once read these words of wisdom by an early Greek philosopher: "He will do great things who first does small things greatly."

FRIDAY— APRIL 21.

THE Lady Of The House was strolling along the street one day when she noticed that there was a queue of stationary traffic. At the head was a lorry which had stopped at a pedestrian crossing.

Several people were running about near the lorry. Had there been an accident? she wondered. Fortunately not, as it turned out.

Beneath the lorry a frightened young sparrow was crouching, and someone was guiding the driver very slowly forward to avoid hurting the bird. Once the sparrow realised that it was safe, it spread its wings and flew off.

What does the Good Book say about God watching over sparrows? Not a single one falls to the ground without God knowing — and caring.

SATURDAY — APRIL 22.

I WAS once shown a selection of Spanish proverbs and asked to say which was my favourite. An impossible task but I found this one fitting for any occasion: "Don't speak unless you can improve on the silence."

SUNDAY — APRIL 23.

THEN Nathan said unto David, Do all that is in thine heart: for God is with thee.

Chronicles I 17:2

MONDAY — APRIL 24.

DO manners matter? Of course they do. We all like to see a door held open for an elderly person, or a seat given up on a bus. I have seen the Lady of the House come home glowing after witnessing good manners.

A friend who is well travelled tells me that the further he goes from "civilisation", the better the manners, that it's sometimes amongst people in the poorest countries that he finds the most politeness.

"Often," he says, "they have nothing — nothing but their good manners."

Now there is something to ponder over.

TUESDAY — APRIL 25.

"OH dear," said Sally, "for weeks I've been thinking what an unfriendly neighbour I had, only to discover today that he has a hearing problem. That'll teach me not to be so quick to judge."

I felt sorry for her, for often it's easy to make mistakes and all too hard to admit, even to ourselves, that we have made them. Happily, Sally was brave enough to do so, and wise enough to start making amends. As the saying puts it: "No matter how far you've gone on the wrong road, never be afraid to turn round."

WEDNESDAY — APRIL 26.

THE poet Longfellow called them the "forget-me-nots of the angels". For Thomas Carlyle they were "street lamps of the City of God".

Stars have always brought out the best in writers. Matthew Arnold was inspired to plead, "Still, let me, as I gaze on you, feel my soul becoming vast like you."

In many places there is now so much artificial light the stars are scarcely visible. If you are lucky enough to be where they still shine, take time tonight to wonder at their beauty.

THURSDAY — APRIL 27.

THE story is told of a woman who wrote to her friend and asked if she would pray for her. This was the friend's reply:

I said a prayer for you today
And know He must have heard —
I felt the answer in my heart
Although He spoke no word.
I didn't ask for wealth or fame
(I knew you wouldn't mind),
I asked Him to send treasures
Of a far more lasting kind.
I asked that He'd be near to you
At the start of each new day,
To grant you health and blessings
And friends to share your way.
I asked for happiness for you
In all things great and small —
But it was for His loving care
I prayed the most of all.

FRIDAY — APRIL 28.

ELIZABETH deals with people who can, on occasion, be difficult. It can be a stressful job yet she always remains calm and polite.

When I asked her how she does it, she smiled and pointed to the poster behind her desk: "Keep your words soft and tender. Tomorrow you may have to eat them!"

SATURDAY — APRIL 29.

"YOU know," said the Lady of the House one afternoon, looking up from her book, "next time I'm tempted to judge by appearance, I shall remember the baobab tree."

I obviously looked a little puzzled, for she elaborated: "The baobab tree must be one of the ugliest trees in the world, but its usefulness is beyond measure. It can survive in the most arid deserts, its bark can be made into rope, its pulp is good for the blood, its seeds provide fertiliser and its flowers are used for decoration, food and medicine.

"So next time I feel like dismissing something or someone just because they're not outwardly attractive, I shall remind myself of the baobab tree."

Well, it's an unusual sort of memory-jogger, but I certainly agree with her sentiments!

SUNDAY — APRIL 30.

AND all the earth sought to Solomon, to hear his wisdom, which God had put in his heart.

Kings I 10:24

May

HAPPINESS IS . . .

*N*OT *across some distant hill*
  Or far away beyond a star,
Happiness is close beside you
  Happiness is where you are.

Not on some exotic isle,
  But maybe somewhere down the lane,
Happiness is unexpected
  Like a rainbow after rain.

Happiness is peace of mind
  To warm the heart and smooth the brow,
The love of home, the joy of friends,
  Happiness is here and now!

                    Iris Hesselden.

I CAUGHT sight of these amusing words on a poster outside a church one day when I was out for a walk:

"The world is full of willing people . . . Some willing to work, and the rest willing to let them. Which are you?"

Which, indeed! Food for thought for us all today.

WEDNESDAY — MAY 3.

OUR old friend Mary was telling us about her neighbour's little boy who, while visiting with his mother, had suddenly noticed a china ornament of the three wise monkeys standing on her mantelpiece.

"He couldn't understand why they had their paws over their eyes, ears and mouth, until I explained their names —See no Evil, Hear no Evil and Speak no Evil. But I suppose," she admitted, "these ornaments are probably rather old fashioned now."

Old fashioned or not, I can't help reflecting that in times when it often seems more and more acceptable to spend time gossiping about the frailties of our fellow men, more wise monkeys in the world might make it a better place!

THURSDAY — MAY 4.

A FRIEND was visiting a big modern office with many mirror-effect panels when he caught sight of himself looking rather serious.

Seeing the reflection, there for all to view, he was reminded of these words by the 19th-century writer William Makepeace Thackeray:

"The world is a looking-glass that gives back to every man the reflection of his own face. Frown at it, and it will in turn, look sourly upon you.

"Laugh at or with it, and it is a jolly, kind companion."

Words to reflect on, I'm sure, in those moments when we forget that our image, sad or happy, is on show to everyone.

A GOLDEN MOMENT

FRIDAY — MAY 5.

SIR Humphrey Davy was responsible for numerous advances in science but is best remembered for inventing the safety lamp which not only lights the way for miners but warns them of dangerous gases.

He could have made a lot of money from his invention if he had patented it but he refused to do so. When asked why he replied, "My sole object was to serve the cause of humanity. If I have succeeded, I am amply rewarded . . . More wealth could not increase either my fame or my happiness."

This brilliant and generous man died in 1829 aged only 50.

SATURDAY — MAY 6.

LIFE can be demanding — we all need quiet moments to reflect and to dream a little, to keep in touch with ourselves, to smile at pleasant thoughts and happy memories, and in these words of the poet William Blake:

To see a world in a grain of sand
And a Heaven in a wild flower
Hold infinity in the palm of your hand
And Eternity in an hour . . .

We then return to our daily lives refreshed, all the more able to achieve what we set out to do.

SUNDAY — MAY 7.

HEAVEN and earth shall pass away: but my words shall not pass away.

Mark 13:31

MONDAY — MAY 8.

THE Rev. Henry Francis Lyte was born in 1793 in the village of Ednam, near Kelso in the Scottish Borders. He did not know whether to be a doctor or enter the church. He decided to follow the latter course, and in the sun and rain of life expressed his faith by the writing of numerous hymns. Two of the best known are the joyous "Praise My Soul, The King Of Heaven", inspired by the 103rd Psalm, and "Abide With Me".

The evening Henry wrote the words and composed the music for "Abide With Me" he was at a crisis point in his life and seriously ill, but he held fast to his faith, and after taking what was to be his last church service in the little fishing port of Brixham in Devon, he went for a quiet walk by the sea, and returned to his study to compose in less than an hour the much-loved "Abide With Me", which echoes so many people's faith.

Henry Francis Lyte died in 1847 and is buried in Nice. His hymns live on many generations later.

TUESDAY — MAY 9.

BE full of enthusiasm in what you do. The best thinkers in the world say it is the light that leads and the strength that lifts people on and up.

Here is one of my favourite thoughts on the subject, from the pen of the writer Dale Carnegie:

"If you believe in what you are doing, then let nothing hold you up in your work. Most of the great achievements of the world have been done against seeming impossibilities."

WEDNESDAY — MAY 10.

*M*Y fountain pen is far from new,
   I've had it many years,
It's been with me through times of joy,
   Of happiness and tears.
It's written letters by the score,
   Penned notes to say I care,
Said sorry that I couldn't come,
   And told folks, "I'll be there!"
It's written cheques and filled in forms,
   Its service never ends,
So what's my favourite use of all?
   It's writing to my friends!

Margaret Ingall.

THURSDAY — MAY 11.

VISITING Sam one afternoon, I found him surveying a camellia with satisfaction. "It has made a good recovery from frost damage, this one," he informed me. "Isn't it funny how plants can be just like folk?"

I looked surprised, and he grinned. "Oh, not in susceptibility to frost," he hastened to reassure me, "but in the way they react to events around them. Some seem to actually thrive on adversity, while others do much better left in peace. Some would take over the whole border if given the chance, while others need just a little coaxing to bring out the best in them."

I had to agree — and was glad to do so, for what a glorious garden of a world we live in. It may never be quite as perfect as we want it to be, but it will never be dull.

FRIDAY — MAY 12.

I WAS walking along the main street one day when I realised that my companion was humming quietly to herself. She smiled, a little self-consciously, then said: "Sorry, but I love that song. I always sing it to myself when I feel a little down."

"Please continue," I told her.

I was reminded of the Rodgers and Hammerstein musical "The King And I", and remembered the inspiring words of Anna as she bursts into these tuneful words: "Whenever I feel afraid, I hold my head erect, and whistle a happy tune, so no-one will suspect I'm afraid."

SATURDAY — MAY 13.

IT'S easy to feel pleased with yourself if you are a success, but what if you have tried something and failed?

These lines have encouraged many whose hopes had been dashed, and perhaps someone reading this will take new heart from them:

Failure doesn't mean you are a failure;
It does mean you haven't yet succeeded.
Failure doesn't mean you should give up;
It does mean you should try harder.
Failure doesn't mean you will never make it;
It does mean it will take a little longer.

SUNDAY — MAY 14.

FOR where two or three are gathered together in my name, there am I in the midst of them.

Matthew 18:20

MONDAY — MAY 15.

YOUNG Tom was attempting, with furrowed brow, to describe the lollipop lady who works at his infant school.

"She's just like a lighthouse," he explained at last triumphantly.

"You mean she's very tall and thin?" questioned his bemused grandmother.

"No," said Tom. "I mean that she stops us running into danger!"

Like Tom's grandmother I, too, laughed at that story. When talking about fellow humans, some things are a great deal more important than mere physical appearance.

TUESDAY — MAY 16.

OUR friends Ian and Dorothy invited two friends to visit one evening and the conversation and happy memories were soon flowing in abundance.

Later, looking at the clock, everyone remarked: "Goodness, is it that time already?" The hours had sped by, and no-one had noticed.

This happens when good friends meet. There is always so much to talk about, isn't there?

Such happy get-togethers remind me of what the novelist Louisa May Alcott said about the occasions when she had friends round for tea. The visits proved so enjoyable that she had to ask them not to rush home too soon.

"I've realised," she said, "that the most charming word in a friend's vocabulary is the one that reads: stay."

WEDNESDAY — MAY 17.

I CAME across this quotation and it reminded me so much of a person I used to know. You, too, will probably know someone who tries to "meet trouble half way".

Never bear more than one kind of trouble at a time. Some people bear three — "all they have had, all they have now and all they expect to have".

It's such a pity that some folk are unable to put past trouble behind them. After all, to go into the future actively looking for it must be rather self-defeating.

If we could all learn to live one day at a time and deal with that day's problems, I think we would all get along much better.

THURSDAY — MAY 18.

SECRET DOOR

WHAT a strange and lovely thing
To think a simple flower,
By the perfume in its depths
Should have the hidden power —
To draw us back into the past
Beyond a secret door,
To relive in memory
Our childhood days once more.

Kathleen Gillum.

FRIDAY — MAY 19.

BUT be not thou far from me, O Lord: O my strength, haste thee to help me.

Psalms 22:19

SATURDAY — MAY 20.

WHEN Geoff first started landscape painting, success didn't come easily. At first his enthusiasm far outstripped his skills, but he kept on trying until at last he was able to produce results that pleased him. Nowadays his talents have turned him into something of a local celebrity yet he remains the same pleasant, unpretentious person that he always was.

"I was still young," he told me, "when I first read Kipling's poem 'If', but the quote: 'If you can meet with Triumph and Disaster, and treat those two impostors just the same' have often helped me to keep a sense of perspective on life."

A sentiment worth remembering — and not just for the poets or painters among us.

SUNDAY — MAY 21.

AND in that day shall ye say, Praise the Lord, call upon his name, declare his doings among the people, make mention that his name is exalted.   Isaiah 12:4

MONDAY — MAY 22.

IF you were to stand in the street with a message on a placard, what would you want it to say? That was the question put to our local church group. Not more than two words were allowed.

"Slow down" was one suggestion. "Peace please" was another. But by far the most popular choice was the one word "Love".

Yes, it's still the most precious thing in the world, isn't it?

TUESDAY — MAY 23.

I HAVE come across many different words of advice about how to do our work well. However, I think the best, and the simplest, message is contained in this passage which Martin Luther King Jr. gives in his book "Facing The Challenge Of A New Age In Philosophy":

"If it falls to your lot to be a street sweeper, make sure you sweep the streets like Michelangelo painted memorable pictures, like Shakespeare wrote fine poetry, like Beethoven composed great music.

"Sweep your street so well that all will have to pause and say, 'Here lived a great sweeper, one who swept his piece of the world so well'."

WEDNESDAY — MAY 24.

MANY tributes in verse have been made to trees. Here is an unusual one from the days of wooden ships:

What do we do when we plant a tree?
We plant a ship that will cross the sea;
We plant the mast to carry the sails,
We plant the planks to withstand the gales,
The keel, the keelson, the beam, the knee,
We plant a ship when we plant a tree.

THURSDAY — MAY 25.

OFTEN I think one word we could remove from our speech and thoughts is "me". It's one of the smallest words, but it often causes the greatest damage.

FRIDAY— MAY 26.

WORDS

WORDS are waves that pound the sand
And travel far away.
Words are trees that rock and sway
And shake off all their leaves.
Words are whispers in your ear
That echo in the mind.
Words are swallows flying high
That never touch the ground.
Words are clouds in the sky
That always change their shape.
Words are footsteps in the snow
That melt into the night
Words are kisses on the cheek
That greet and say good-bye.
Words are smiles from the heart
That help you to your feet.

David Elder.

SATURDAY — MAY 27.

I WANT to share with you today these thoughts about a smile.

A smile is daylight to the discouraged, sunshine to the sad.

A smile costs nothing but creates much.

SUNDAY — MAY 28.

THEREFORE whosoever heareth these sayings of mine, and doeth them, I will liken him unto a wise man, which built his house upon a rock.

Matthew 7:24

ALL TOGETHER NOW!

MONDAY — MAY 29.

I HEARD a broadcaster say to one of his listeners: "Thank you for your time."

Do we value the hours and minutes we use up each day? I offer you this thought from the writings of John Oliver Killens:

"Life is a short walk. There is so little time and so much living to achieve."

Let's make the most of each day.

TUESDAY — MAY 30.

NELL is one of the best kind of neighbours — always friendly and willing to help. Her attitude reminds me of a little poem I once read:

Always be a listener
If someone needs your ear,
Assist with others' burdens
And if you can, give cheer.
But when you've sat and listened
Don't tell what you've been told,
For a friend who never gossips
Is a friend of purest gold!

WEDNESDAY — MAY 31.

THE Lady of the House came up with two rather interesting quotations one day. Although from different times and different countries, they are encouragingly like-minded:

From Alexander Dumas we have: "Friendship consists in forgetting what one gives and remembering what one receives", while from Winston Churchill: "We make a living by what we get; we make a life by what we give."

June

NOW and then I like to remind myself of a quotation from "Alice Through The Looking Glass".

It's the one where the Queen says to Alice: "Sometimes I've believed as many as six impossible things before breakfast!"

And why not I ask myself. The world is full of wonderful and seemingly impossible things, often discovered when least expected.

If we feel that life is getting a little humdrum, let's try to believe in the exciting and the apparently impossible. It will give a lift to the morning and set us up for the day.

LOOKING forward to something is part of human nature, but we can carry it to extremes. Many people seem to live in the future, just as others appear to live in the past.

Living each day to the best of our ability is surely what really matters. As the nineteenth-century Scottish writer and historian Thomas Carlyle expressed it well:

"Our grand business undoubtedly is not to see what lies dimly at a distance but to do what lies clearly at hand."

SATURDAY — JUNE 3.

THEY say that genius is an infinite capacity for taking pains. Paderewski, the great violinist, evidently believed this.

When he was young he spent long hours in practice. At the height of his fame he was complimented by Queen Victoria:

"Mr Paderewski, you are a genius."

"That may be, Ma'am," he replied. "But before I was a genius, I was a drudge!"

SUNDAY — JUNE 4.

AND early in the morning he came again into the temple, and all the people came unto him; and he sat down, and taught them.

John 8:2

MONDAY — JUNE 5.

NATURE'S PAINTBOX

*A PALETTE rich in wonder
  Earth's colours on display
Pink and purple mountains
  And the green-of-forest days.
Shell tint in stone-clad walling
  Haze of the golden sun
Fish leaping in the water
  A silver ballet spun.
Blissful blues in the lucent sky
  Blushed rose on the wanton sea
The joys of nature's paintbox
  A wondrous filigree.*

Dorothy McGregor.

TUESDAY — JUNE 6.

WE had the pleasure the other day of looking through Catherine's autograph book dating from her younger days. It was a book of real friendship with not one signature of a "personality" in sight.

The pages were filled with contributions, both serious and amusing, from family and friends. One page signed "Jayne" especially caught my attention; it was beautifully decorated with coloured inks, and centred on the page were the words — "hold a true friend with both your hands".

Wise words indeed. Catherine told us that she and Jayne were still good friends, and the words Jayne had written in her autograph book were, in fact, a Nigerian proverb.

WEDNESDAY — JUNE 7.

FROM over the centuries come these wishes of Eusebius, an early Bishop of Caesarea:

*May I be no man's enemy, and may I be the
    friend of that which is eternal and abides.
May I never quarrel with those nearest to me,
    and if I do, may I be reconciled quickly.
May I love, seek, and attain only what is good.
May I wish for all men's happiness and
    envy no-one.
May I never rejoice in the ill fortune of someone
    who has wronged me.
May I win no victory that harms either me or
    my opponent.*

Not a bad creed for today, is it?

THURSDAY — JUNE 8.

WE were once visiting a beautiful part of north-east England and came across a welcoming guest house. It was clean and comfortable, the views delightful and the owners friendly.

As the Lady of the House and I entered the dining-room, I noticed above the door a small plaque with this quotation from the Bible:

As for me and my house, we will serve the Lord.

Joshua 24:15

There were visitors there that week from the United States, France, Canada and Australia and I thought, what better way to serve the Lord than to offer hospitality and a warm welcome?

That is something we can all do in our own small way, whether we are on holiday or not.

FRIDAY — JUNE 9.

MOTHER Teresa was well known for her works of charity among the poor and needy in India. Often when we consider how some individuals have filled their lives with such selfless devotion to others, it can make us feel unworthy. Few people will ever achieve what she did; few of us will ever touch so many lives. However, take courage and inspiration from Mother Teresa's own wise words.

"We can do no great things — only small things with great love."

We may not touch a nation, but if we care enough we reach out to others, one at a time, and we will make a difference.

SATURDAY — JUNE 10.

ARE you in a rut? This question was asked one day by Monica when she found a business card with these memorable words on the back:

If you always go where you've always gone,
If you always do what you've always done,
You will always be
What you've always been.

Whatever our age, fresh perspectives can come by making a minor change to routine, or indeed, taking up a new interest or hobby can open many doors.

SUNDAY — JUNE 11.

I WAITED patiently for the Lord; and he inclined unto me, and heard my cry.

Psalms 40:1

MONDAY — JUNE 12.

OUR friend Paula was facing a difficult Monday at the start of another week when she received this e-mailed tip from a friend.

"Get yourself a pen and paper and write down — now! — three goals for today that you know you can achieve. Put them at the very top of your daily 'to-do' list. And get them done first.

"The satisfaction you will feel after completing three jobs effortlessly will set you up for the entire day and gradually, harder tasks will start to look much simpler."

She took the friendly instructions to heart and had a good day — and some even better ones thereafter!

TUESDAY — JUNE 13.

THE great statesman, Lord Shaftesbury, carried an old gold watch about with him. It had seen better days but he proudly showed it to people, saying, "This belonged to the best friend I ever had."

The friend was the family housekeeper who, when he was a boy, told him his first Bible stories. Every time he looked at the watch he remembered what she had taught him.

WEDNESDAY — JUNE 14.

LIKE all of us I associate the name Walt Disney with adding fun and enjoyment to life. His amusement parks in the United States and Europe keep thousands of parents and their families entertained.

Walt, who lived from 1901 to 1966, genuinely had the welfare and the happiness of people in mind as well as business interests. He once said, "I would rather entertain and hope that people learned something than educate people and hope they were entertained."

I have also read these "Disney-isms":

"Every child is born blessed with a vivid imagination. But just as muscles grow flabby with disuse, so the bright imagination of a child pales in later years if he ceases to exercise it."

"There is more treasure in books than in all the pirates' loot on Treasure Island and, best of all, you can enjoy these riches every day of your life."

Walt Disney's "Kingdoms Of Fun" continue to make the world a brighter place.

THURSDAY — JUNE 15.

I HAVE collected many sayings about friendship over the years, but here is one of the best and, perhaps, one of the less well known:

"There is only one thing better than making a new friend, and that is keeping an old one."

How true!

FRIDAY — JUNE 16.

FLEETING YEAR

COLD January creeps along,
  Dark February, too.
Then March and April skipping by
  Provide a brighter view.
In May and June the beauty grows
  The time now flowing on,
And suddenly the longest day
  Has simply come and gone!

July and August touch the hills
  And colour plant and fern,
Whilst here and there we notice leaves
  Beginning now to turn.
September and October make
  A magical display,
The year is moving faster still
  As weeks all slip away.

And so the months keep passing by
  And so the time takes wing,
Don't miss the beauty and the joy
  The fleeting year can bring!

                    Iris Hesselden.

SATURDAY — JUNE 17.

OUR friend Elizabeth is a great one for country rambles. On a good day she will walk for miles, but if the weather is bad or the trail overgrown, then she finds the effort rather more challenging. While on one of her not-so-easy expeditions, she came up with this verse. The sentiments apply to almost any endeavour!

The path to success isn't easy
The path to success isn't straight
You may have to jump a few puddles
You may need to clamber a gate
But if you keep doggedly trying
And refuse to give up or turn round
Why then, your endeavour's rewarded
And at last journey's end will be found.

SUNDAY — JUNE 18.

VERILY, verily, I say unto you, He that believeth in me hath everlasting life.

John 6:47

MONDAY — JUNE 19.

WHAT is civilisation? Is it having all the most up-to-date technology, the most modern homes and labour-saving gadgets?

Ralph Waldo Emerson said that the true test of a civilisation was not the size of its cities but the kind of people it turned out. Another definition I like is this one: "civilisation — the slow process of learning to be kind."

Yes, that is civilisation, learning to be kind to one another.

TUESDAY — JUNE 20.

*S*ILENCE PLEASE! We often come across these words, usually printed in large letters, in libraries and other public areas where people are reading quietly or studying.

Another official instruction, often found in centuries-old cathedrals of the world, reminds visitors: *This is a Quiet Place.*

Our friend, Helen, was delighted one day to visit a children's ward in a city hospital and see these words:

Shh! Shh! . . .

The Loveliest Sound in the World.

Now, isn't that the kind of informal request which brings out the best in all of us? Remember, you don't have to shout at people to get them to do something.

WEDNESDAY — JUNE 21.

MASTERPIECE

I MAY not be a sculptor
Who chisels works of art
I may not be a painter
Whose brushstrokes touch the heart,
I may not use a pencil
With talent or prowess,
I may not wield a crayon,
With guaranteed success,
But if you see my garden
You'll surely know it's true,
With a little help from heaven,
I've a masterpiece on view.

Margaret Ingall.

THURSDAY — JUNE 22.

STUDENTS at Villanova University in Pennsylvania still talk of the graduation day speech given in 1999 by Anna Quindlen, the Pulitzer Prizewinning author.

"Life is the best thing ever, and we have no business taking it for granted," she told them. "It is so easy to waste our lives, to take for granted the colour of our kids' eyes, the way the melody in a symphony rises and falls and disappears and rises again.

"Get a real life, not a pursuit of the next promotion, the bigger pay-cheque, the larger house. Get a life in which you notice the smell of salt water pushing itself on a breeze, a life in which you stop and watch how a red-tailed hawk circles over the water, or the way a baby scowls with concentration when she tries to pick up a sweet with her thumb and first finger."

Wise words to keep in mind.

FRIDAY — JUNE 23.

OUR friend Beth is one of the busiest people we know. One of her hobbies is writing poetry, and this one could not be more apt:

I can't hold back the minutes,
They fly by much too fast,
I can't postpone the future,
Nor yet retrieve the past.
But one thing I can do
To make the present shine
Is polish up the here and now,
For that's forever mine!

SATURDAY — JUNE 24.

IN Norway there's a folk tale explaining why the dog has a wet nose. During the voyage of the Ark, the vessel sprang a leak, and the dog — who had become a good friend to Noah during the first two weeks of the journey — obligingly put his nose into the gap between the planks.

It was a perfect fit and everyone reached journey's end in complete safety. This story also helps to explain, I'm sure, the strength of that long-established bond between our best friend and ourselves.

SUNDAY — JUNE 25.

AND when they were come, and had gathered the church together, they rehearsed all that God had done with them, and how he had opened the door of faith unto the Gentiles.

Acts 14:27

MONDAY — JUNE 26.

ANDY is head of a well-known charity organisation. Once he had to find someone to fill an important post dealing with vulnerable people.

He invited four applicants to lunch in a restaurant and after the meal he announced who was to get the job.

"Why did you choose me?" the person asked, clearly puzzled.

"It was easy," came the reply. "You were the only one who said 'thank you' every time to the waiter."

TUESDAY — JUNE 27.

LAST week Beverley missed the bus. She'd been intending to spend a day in the nearest city but when she saw the bus leave without her decided instead to catch the next one, wherever it might be going.

"And, do you know, I had a lovely day," she told me afterwards. "I found myself being driven through so many pretty villages to a nearby market town. There I had a wander round, before catching a different bus home, which took me back by another attractive route."

I'm glad she enjoyed her outing. Life may not always take us on the road we'd intended but if, like Beverley, we're prepared to regard a change of plan as an opportunity, then who knows what unexpected pleasures we may discover on the way?

WEDNESDAY— JUNE 28.

TODAY I want to look at faults. No, not to complain about other people's! I'm thinking of the poet Goethe who said he looked around him and saw no faults that he might not have himself.

Another writer, La Rochefoucauld, observed that if we had no faults, we would not take such delight in criticising others. Then the poet Tennyson wrote, "He is all fault who hath no fault at all."

Finally, I am reminded of lines by Alexander Pope from one of my favourite prayers:
Teach me to feel another's woe,
To hide the fault I see.

THURSDAY — JUNE 29.

THESE lines from a favourite contributor seem to capture perfectly the start of another precious day:

MORNING

Clear — the dawn,
The waiting hour;

Clear— the air,
Horizon's rim;

Swift — the hues,
The sunbeam's ray;

Swift — the rush,
The onward tide;

Joy — the song
The birds now trill;

Joy — begins
This new born-day.

Elizabeth Gozney.

FRIDAY — JUNE 30.

DO you remember the actor Sir C. Aubrey Smith? His craggy face graced many British and American films and he was invariably asked to play the part of a dignified but humorous gentleman, roles which he played to perfection.

He loved the game of cricket and prominent on his desk was a notice which said: "Play the game of life with a straight bat and never blame the umpire."

Advice that was typical of the man.

TRANQUIL WATERS

July

I WONDER how many of you are familiar with the novel "Three Men In A Boat"? Author Jerome K. Jerome's account of a river trip undertaken one Summer in the 1880s continues to enchant; a much-loved classic, a lyrical, yet also gloriously funny book, frequently featuring the author as the butt of his own comedy.

Perhaps few people know that as well as being a great humorist, Jerome was also a thoughtful, religious and courageous man. Although well into his fifties at the time of the Great War, he still chose to enlist as a volunteer ambulance driver — a brave decision, one which undoubtedly shortened his life.

Happily, he did live long enough to see how much pleasure his writing brought to the world. As he himself wrote, we all need "time to drink in life's sunshine" and to me "Three Men In A Boat" is the perfect brew.

A ND when they had prayed, the place was shaken where they were assembled together; and they were all filled with the Holy Ghost, and they spake the word of God with boldness.

Acts 4:31

MONDAY — JULY 3.

OUR lecturer friend Bill was looking very pleased with himself. "The Summer holidays have just started," he explained. "So for now, my days are all my own. And yet," he continued, "the funny thing is, that by the time Autumn arrives, I know I'll be really looking forward to going back. There's something about a new beginning that always excites me."

I knew exactly what he meant, for whether it's the start of a new year, a new project, or simply a new page in a diary, there is indeed something exhilarating about a fresh beginning. It's a chance to make good our previous mistakes, to try out fresh ideas, to try harder and do better.

Now, if only we could bring that enthusiasm to the start of every day that dawns . . . Well, we can but try!

TUESDAY — JULY 4.

"HAVE you ever noticed," asked our old friend Mary, "how a garden can sometimes be just like a time machine?"

I had to admit I hadn't but as she showed me round, I began to see what she meant. "The smell of lavender," she said, "takes me straight back to my grandmother — it was her favourite scent.

"Whenever I pick an apple, I'm back harvesting fruit with my father. When I touch lily of the valley, I'm holding my wedding bouquet, and when I see daisies, I'm sitting in a meadow helping my children make daisy chains. My garden brings so many memories alive, I always love working in it."

WEDNESDAY — JULY 5.

AT the age of twelve, Peter Grant was fluent in both written and spoken Gaelic, but had little knowledge of English. By the time he was twenty-three he was running the family croft in Strathspey in Scotland and tending his sheep, every spare minute spent book in hand, so intent was he on self-education.

He joined the local Baptist congregation and for the next 60 years was a persuasive preacher, his services well attended. In addition to becoming minister of his own church in Grantown-on-Spey, he continued as a travelling agent for the Baptist Mission, covering thousands of miles all over the Highlands on foot.

His hymns, written to replace the sometimes bawdy songs sung at local weddings, proved popular and earned him the name *Padruig Grannd Nan Oran* (Peter Grant Of The Songs) and when asked where he had been educated, his answer was typically modest: "Between the shafts of the plough."

THURSDAY — JULY 6.

OUR friend Joanne once gave us this advice about how to handle conversation:

"Learn to shut up!" she said. "It's always wise to listen. God gave us two ears and one mouth, so He must have meant us to do twice as much listening as talking.

"Just give yourself the 'Shut Up' command," she continued, "and let wise and experienced ones do the talking."

FRIDAY — JULY 7.

THE other day I read with great pleasure these cheerful and inspiring words of the late Jawaharlal Nehru, the great Indian statesman, who was the first Prime Minister of independent India:

"We live in a wonderful world that is full of beauty, charm and adventure. There is no end to the adventures we can have if only we seek them with our eyes open."

Words which make a wonderful thought for today, and for every day of our lives. I wish you all many happy adventures!

SATURDAY — JULY 8.

THE world is great and glorious
  Both wonderful and strange,
From the darkest, deepest ocean
  To the highest mountain range.
Exciting and mysterious
  With places yet unclaimed,
From lonely tropic islands
  To jungle still untamed.

From the icebergs of the Arctic
  To the burning desert sands,
There's beauty made for sharing
  In many far-off lands.
The world can still be glorious
  When centuries have gone,
If man will strive to keep it safe
  For those who follow on!

                    Iris Hesselden.

SUNDAY — JULY 9.

EVERY word of God is pure: he is a shield unto them that put their trust in him.

Proverbs 30:5

MONDAY — JULY 10.

OUR friend Michelle's ten-year-old daughter was telling her mother that she loved her "like a circle".

"At first I didn't know what she meant," said Michelle. "I was intrigued, of course, but her train of thought eluded me."

"No end, no beginning. It just is," came the explanation later.

These words from a small child filled her with indescribable joy. For mothers everywhere "like a circle" surely says it all.

TUESDAY — JULY 11.

THERE are, it's often said, two ways of looking at most things, and this surely applies to the ageing process. Too often we see it as a somewhat negative development — a narrowing of outlook, a shutting down of all that makes life interesting.

Personally, I much prefer the American poet Henry Wadsworth Longfellow's view:

Age is opportunity no less
Than youth itself, though in another dress,
And as the evening twilight fades away,
The sky is filled with stars, invisible by day.

And, after all, who doesn't enjoy a little star gazing?

WEDNESDAY — JULY 12.

SUNFLOWERS prove a great inspiration to those who see them, sprouting up tall and bright in their brilliant yellow or vivid orange colours.

The American poet Albert Bigelow Paine, in a book of poems published in 1926, wrote of the wide "golden fields of Kansas where the sunflowers bloom". The tall stems and large yellow-rayed flower heads are an inspiring symbol of strength.

A strong and healthy sunflower, and sunbeams winking at us are always inspiring. St Francis of Assisi wrote: "A single sunbeam is enough to drive away many shadows."

May your day shine with sunflowers or sunbeams. You are fortunate indeed if you have both.

THURSDAY — JULY 13.

TIME, it has often been observed, is one of the great enigmas of life, and over the years many men and women have spoken wise — and sometimes not so wise — words on the subject. Here are a couple of my favourites, which may not have done much to enlighten me, but certainly made me smile:

"Tomorrow is the busiest day of the week."

Spanish proverb.

"Time is nature's way of stopping everything happening at once."   John Archibald Wheeler.

Now, I think I need a few moments to think about these!

FRIDAY — JULY 14.

DESIGNER'S ART

RAINBOWS seen through Summer showers
Velvet faces of the flowers,
Frost crystals reflecting light
Snowflakes on a Winter's night.
Symmetry of honeycomb
Sunshine sparkling on sea foam.
Gossamer of silken threads
Form cartwheels of the spider webs.
Animals of every size
Insects, birds and butterflies.
This tapestry of art and skill
Is wrought by the Designer's will.

Kathleen Gillum.

SATURDAY — JULY 15.

HERE are some memorable words from the twenty-eighth President of the United States, Woodrow Wilson:

"We are not here merely to make a living. We are here in order to enable the world to live more amply, with greater vision, with a finer spirit of hope and achievement.

"We are here to enrich the world, and we will impoverish ourselves if we forget that errand."

SUNDAY — JULY 16.

HUMBLE yourselves therefore under the mighty hand of God, that he may exalt you in due time: Casting all your care upon him; for he careth for you.

Peter I 5:6-7

FUN OF
THE FAIR

MONDAY — JULY 17.

IT always saddens me when I read the most beautiful words written about someone in their obituary, because so often a person won't have heard these words spoken during their own lifetime.

All too often we undervalue people or take them for granted. But the praise that's expressed in an obituary alone is too late — let's offer it now!

TUESDAY — JULY 18.

IT'S UP TO YOU!

THE University Of Life
    Is quite an institution,
With all of us involved in its
    Distinctive contribution.
Though subjects tend to vary,
    The challenge seems to stress
That with some effort we can gain
    Degrees of Happiness.
                    John M. Robertson.

WEDNESDAY — JULY 19.

THE future author Walter Scott was described by one of his teachers as a hopeless dunce. Louis Pasteur was the slowest learner in his chemistry class. Thomas Edison was pronounced stupid and sent home in disgrace. Winston Churchill was expelled from his Latin class.

Today their names live on while their fellow pupils — and their teachers — are forgotten.

The moral? Don't write off a flower before it has had time to bloom.

THURSDAY — JULY 20.

THE person who is truly happy with his current status in life will not need these timely reminders:

You are only poor when you want more than you have.

He who lives content with little possesses everything.

Contentment is not found in having everything, but in being satisfied with everything we have.

FRIDAY — JULY 21.

WE all know the story of the child Pandora and her secret box. When, against all advice, she opened it, she released all sorts of dreadful ills into the world.

By our prayers we, as it were, open another box and blessings are released, not just for ourselves but for others — indeed, for the whole world.

SATURDAY — JULY 22.

HERE is a humbling thought from Scots writer Maurice Fleming:

"Despite all the progress mankind has made over the centuries, all his discoveries and inventions, the baby born this hour will know nothing of any of it. It will be as if none of it had yet happened.

"Every child's mind is a clean sheet. The world's knowledge is out there, but the long learning process has to begin, for that child as for every other, from a starting point of nothing.

"What that child learns rests with you and me."

SUNDAY — JULY 23.

I AM the vine, ye are the branches: He that abideth in me, and I in him, the same bringeth forth much fruit: for without me ye can do nothing.

John 15:5

MONDAY — JULY 24.

THE Lady of the House was humming as she was doing embroidery, and I quickly recognised the tune.

"Yes," she confirmed, "it's 'You Are The Wind Beneath My Wings'. I really like the way the lyrics recognise that nothing can be achieved without encouragement, and that we should never forget to thank those who give it."

On reflection, I quite agree. Success may not always come in the form of vast recorded music sales, but however large or small, it's always satisfying to those who achieve it, in whichever field.

So next time we have reason to feel pleased with ourselves, let's remember to say our thanks to all those who have supported us. For as we all know, without a little wind to help it fly, even a paper kite would be a flop.

TUESDAY — JULY 25.

I FOUND these thought-provoking words, author unknown, in a parish magazine one Sunday evening:

"Good friends are like stars . . . you don't always see them, but you know they are always there."

WEDNESDAY — JULY 26.

WHEN I opened an old book, these words were on the bookmark that fell out: "A heart filled with anger has no room for love."

For every minute that we are angry, we lose sixty seconds of happiness.

THURSDAY — JULY 27.

WHAT would you say is the most important part of your body?

Some friends were having a discussion about this and Rose said, "The eyes."

"No, the ears," replied Jemima, "so you can enjoy friendly arguments like this!"

Then Agnes, who was probably the oldest person in the room, added, "I think you're both wrong. To me, the most important part is my shoulder.

"Not because it supports my head, but because it can hold the head of a friend or loved one when they cry."

How true! Everybody at some time or another needs a shoulder to cry on and a friend to offer that shoulder. People will sometimes forget what you said and what you did, but people will never forget how you made them feel.

FRIDAY — JULY 28.

HERE are three thoughts to keep in mind today:

A heart that's breaking? Mend it.
A tendency to fret? End it.
A hand's for helping. Lend it!

SATURDAY — JULY 29.

HARRY had been a minister in the same church for several years. When he was retiring, he was touched by the good wishes and thanks expressed by members of the congregation.

One man said, "I will miss your sense of humour." A woman told him, "I will miss your sermons," while another said, I will miss your fine singing voice."

However, the one that moved him most was an elderly man who shook his hand and said quietly, "I will miss you for yourself."

There could be no finer tribute.

SUNDAY — JULY 30.

UNTO thee, O my strength, will I sing: for God is my defence, and the God of my mercy.

Psalms 59:17

MONDAY — JULY 31.

THE WAITING HOUR

THESE things endure whate'er may pass:
The Summer tang of new-mown grass,
The gentle skies, the rising dawn,
And friendship's hand to those forlorn.
Smooth, dappled sunshine after rain,
The quietude of country lane.
A kindly word to those in need,
To build up hope, as flowers seed,
And in the daily round, to find
God's precious gift — contented mind.

Elizabeth Gozney.

August

WHEN Donald finally achieved his ambition of buying a vintage car, he was thrilled. He'd always longed to own one, and loved being able to show it off.

Soon, however, he began to find the joys of ownership lacking a little. "Somehow it didn't feel right," he confessed, "to be driving round all by myself."

As a result, he started offering to give rides in his car, raising funds for all kinds of charities. His journeys are always shared — and his vehicle is pure pleasure to him and his passengers.

His experience reminded me of some words from writer and preacher W.T. Purkiser, who said: "Not what we say about our blessings, but how we use them, is the true measure of our thanksgiving."

Now that really is setting us on the right road!

I CAME across this inspiring thought in a church magazine and I'd like to share it with you today:

Serenity isn't freedom from the storm
But peace within the storm.

HIGHLAND HOME

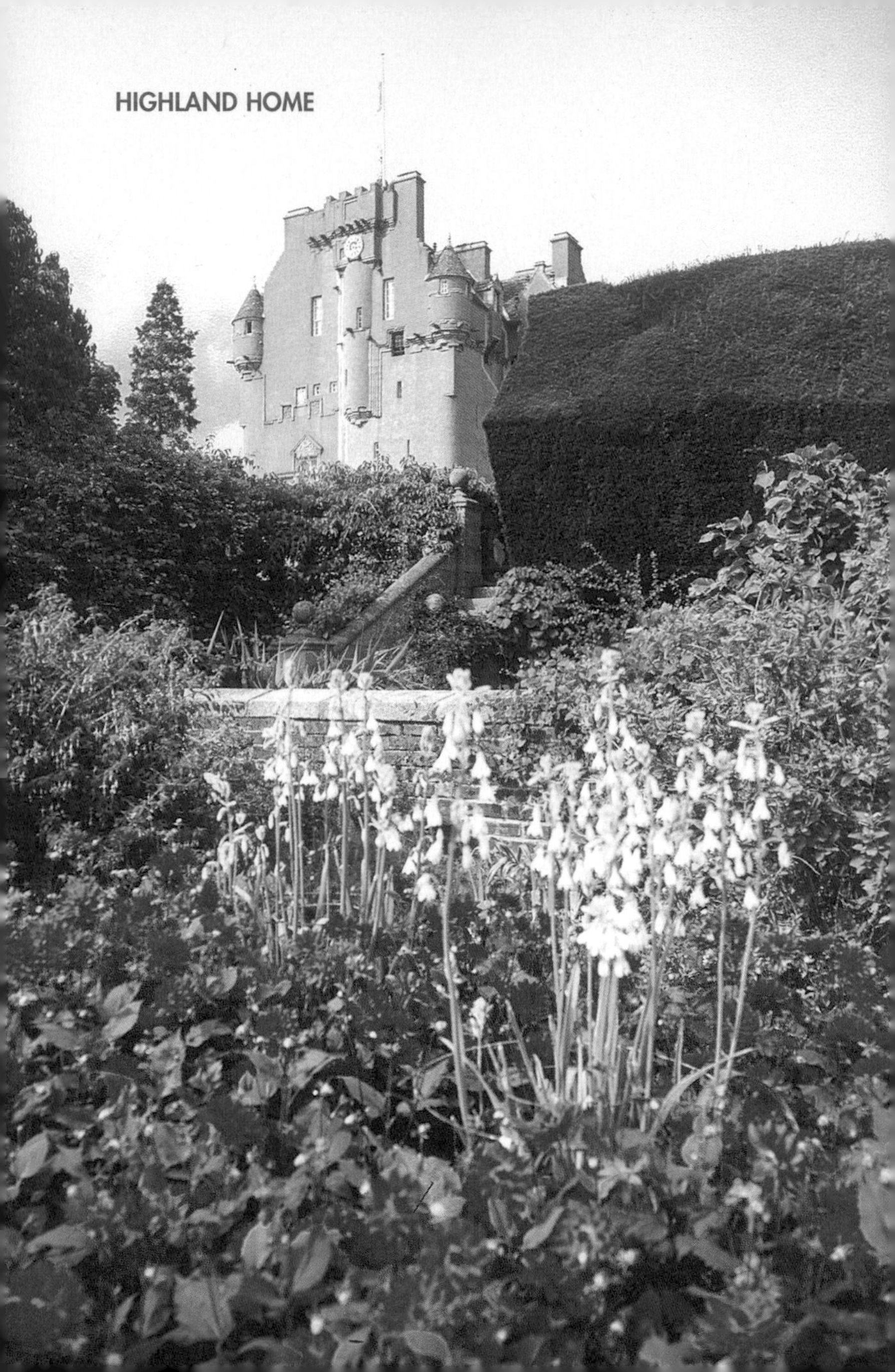

THURSDAY — AUGUST 3.

"I JUST don't have time!" How often do we hear people saying that — and ourselves, too! The truth is that those who really care do have time; they make time for those who need it and aren't selfish about their time.

We may think that we'll lose out by giving our time, but actually we gain by it and there's no better time to give it than right now.

FRIDAY — AUGUST 4.

A CORRESPONDENT sent me this poem "The Divine Weaver" which has brought comfort to many. I'd like to share it with you today:

My life is but a weaving
Between my Lord and me;
I cannot choose the colours
He worketh steadily.

Oftentimes he weaveth sorrow
And I, in foolish pride,
Forget that he seeth the upper,
And I, the underside.

Not 'till the loom is silent
And the shuttles cease to fly,
Shall God unroll the canvas
And explain the reason why.

The dark threads are as needful
In the weavers' skilful hand,
As the threads of gold and silver
In the pattern he has planned.

SATURDAY — AUGUST 5.

SIX-YEAR-OLD Emily loved the sight of rainbows. Her favourite Bible story was about Noah's ark, and the rainbow that came after the flood.

When her father got a new job, several hundred miles from home, fond farewells were said as friends and neighbours waved the family off. Emily threw herself on the back seat of the car and sobbed as if her heart would break. Leaving everything familiar behind her was incredibly painful.

Then, just when she thought her crying would never end, she glanced out of the window and saw a huge rainbow.

And what did that mean to the six-year-old? God was looking after her. He knew how she felt and everything was going to be fine. Slowly she dried her eyes and started to look around her.

When she arrived at her new home she was pleasantly surprised. The cottage was small but pretty, and the garden was enormous.

Emily is in her forties now, but every time she sees a rainbow she thinks back to that day, and has never forgotten its ability to mend a small girl's broken heart.

SUNDAY — AUGUST 6.

AH, Lord God! Behold, thou hast made the heaven and the earth by thy great power and stretched out arm, and there is nothing too hard for thee.

Jeremiah 32:17

MONDAY — AUGUST 7.

NO need to worry if, as you read this, you find yourself alone and with only your thoughts for company. Some of the world's greatest ideas have begun in a small room with just one person thinking and planning.

As our friend David puts it, most of us have more creative thoughts when we are alone. The Lady of the House once brought home these lines, found in a tattered old book of magazine cuttings:

Just stand very still
At a difficult hour,
And wait for a silence within,
You will be led as you wait,
In wisdom and strength,
From too much confusion and din.

TUESDAY — AUGUST 8.

I HAVE always admired the American poet Henry W. Longfellow, the author of memorable poems such as "Hiawatha" and "The Village Blacksmith".

In a busy life up to his death aged seventy-five in 1882, he put his talents and energy into teaching students as a professor of languages at Harvard and other institutions, and kept to a well-organised schedule.

The thought for which I will always remember Henry Longfellow best relates to how we should tackle any new task. "It takes less time," he said, "to do a thing right than it does to explain why you did it wrong."

GREEN, GREEN GRASS
OF HOME

WEDNESDAY — AUGUST 9.

HAVE you ever heard of the carrier pigeon service? It was started during the First World War to send birds to the Front where they were used for carrying messages.

During the Second World War, re-named the National Pigeon Service, it carried on the good work. Thousands of birds were sent into Occupied Europe. They carried questionnaires to be filled in by anyone brave enough to do so, and a great deal of useful information came winging its way back to Britain.

One bird, Mary from Devon, put in five years war service, braving storms, enemy fire, and attacks by birds of prey. For her services she was awarded the Dickin Medal, the animals' VC.

THURSDAY — AUGUST 10.

BESIDE ME

I'VE never seen an angel's flight,
Nor glimpsed a shining wing,
I've never felt an angel's breath,
Or heard an angel sing,
Yet somehow when I'm troubled,
Or lost in doubt and fear,
I seem to sense a presence:
An angel standing near.
And though I still may struggle
On pathways strewn with stone,
I somehow know my burdens
Are never borne alone.

Margaret Ingall.

FRIDAY — AUGUST 11.

TODAY may be "just another day" for many of us, but for our friend, Joe, it will once again be a very special one. Like each and every day from Sunday right through to Saturday.

"Each day, in everyone's life, should be a special one," Joe says. "Never, ever call it an ordinary day. Make today the one when you dress smartly, comb your hair neatly, freshen up, and go out to meet new people, savour fresh ideas.

"Make it a day to do new things. To enjoy more time with your family, perhaps try to concentrate a little less on work. A day to forget worries big and small. To sit in the garden, and savour the fresh air.

"Stop saying 'I would like to . . .' If a thing is worth doing, or seeing, or listening to, doesn't it deserve to be enjoyed this very day? Before the months have passed and it is too late."

SATURDAY — AUGUST 12.

SOME friends were talking one day about gossip and how harmful it can be. We all agreed that it was best not to listen to it and never to pass it on.

One man put it this way: "Why do dogs have so many friends? Because they wag their tails, not their tongues!"

SUNDAY — AUGUST 13.

IN thee, O Lord, do I put my trust; let me never be ashamed: deliver me in thy righteousness.

Psalms 31:1

MONDAY — AUGUST 14.

I AM told that, in Poland, they say that when you are in your forties you have reached the old age of immaturity, and when you reach your fifties you are in the youth of maturity.

It's rather a nice way of looking at the advancing years, isn't it?

TUESDAY — AUGUST 15.

A UTHOR J. B. Priestley was a serious writer. His early volumes of literary criticism may have been what he referred to when he called his writing "grumbling at large". But the man himself was far from serious.

Amongst his many hobbies was an appreciation of art and visits to galleries brought his light-hearted side to the surface. As he said, "I never visit a gallery without wanting to cry to the sad spectators, 'Stop tip-toeing! Have some fun! Find some delight in this place . . . or march straight out!'"

A life-affirming philosophy, I'm sure you'll agree.

WEDNESDAY — AUGUST 16.

H ERE'S advice given to a pupil from a schoolteacher, wise words found in an old autograph book:

Your future lies before you
Like a path of driven snow,
Be careful how you tread it
For every mark will show.

THURSDAY — AUGUST 17.

I READ this "warning" in a church newsletter one day and it made me smile:

"Don't be surprised if you find mistakes. We aim to print something for everyone, and some people are always looking for mistakes."

FRIDAY — AUGUST 18.

JUNE had been ill, so the Lady of the House and I were visiting her when the young girl next door called round with a sponge cake she'd made as a get-well present. June was delighted with both the gift and the thought behind it.

As Hayley departed with a glowing face, June smiled. "I never used to be much good when it came to receiving either favours or presents," she admitted. "I'd feel embarrassed or tongue-tied, and never know what to say. Then I happened to read something by the writer G.B. Stern. She wrote: 'silent gratitude isn't much good to anyone', and these words suddenly made me realise how ungracious my shyness must seem. So now when I'm pleased, I do my best to show it."

SATURDAY — AUGUST 19.

I CAME on these lines, author unknown, and thought them well worth sharing:
Success is failure turned inside out,
The silver tint of the cloud of doubt.
So stick to the fight when you're hardest hit,
It's when things seem worst that you
 mustn't quit!

SUNDAY— AUGUST 20.

GIVE us this day our daily bread.

Matthew 6:11

MONDAY — AUGUST 21.

SUMMER SKIES

TODAY the sun streamed from the sky
  In burning shafts of light,
In splendour and magnificence
  All dazzling, shining bright.
And all of nature sprang to life
  As if by magic hand,
As incandescent radiance
  Poured out across the land.

Suddenly my heart leaps up
  I want to dance and sing,
I feel my spirit lift and soar
  I let my thoughts take wing.
Invigorated by the sun
  I feel fresh hope arise,
As I bask in this sunny burst
  That comes from Summer skies.

Kathleen Gillum.

TUESDAY — AUGUST 22.

WHEN, as a child, Anna tried to do too many things too quickly, her grandmother used to say, "Take your time. The Lord didn't do it all in one day. What makes you think you can?"

Sound advice for us all in these times of rush and bustle.

WEDNESDAY — AUGUST 23.

HERE'S a thought for today, from the writer Thomas Hughes:

"Blessed are those who have the gift of making friends, for it is one of God's best gifts. It involves many things but, above all, the power of going out of one's self, and appreciating whatever is noble and loving in another."

THURSDAY — AUGUST 24.

ONE of the hymns I always enjoy singing is that old favourite, "Father, hear the prayer we offer". Before being turned into a hymn, these verses were originally penned as a poem by a nineteenth-century doctor's wife, the delightfully-named Mrs Love Maria Willis. Whether read, spoken or sung there is a simple directness in her request for heavenly assistance:

Be our Strength in hours of weakness,
In our wanderings be our Guide,
Through endeavour, failure, danger,
Father, be Thou at our side.

Words to bring comfort for many years to come.

FRIDAY — AUGUST 25.

"WASTE not, want not" is a familiar phrase, but our friend Ellen's mother had a charming way of expressing the sentiment.

After breakfast she would say, "Don't throw these crumbs away. That could make a good breakfast for a chaffinch!"

SATURDAY — AUGUST 26.

A LITTLE girl and her mother were alone in their country cottage when the mother took ill during the night. Although dark outside, her daughter at once made her way down the valley to seek help.

Her mother later recovered and asked her daughter, "Were you not frightened going all that way alone in the dark?"

"No," replied the girl, "for the moon came with me."

With it in the sky for company she was unafraid.

SUNDAY — AUGUST 27.

T HEN said Jesus to them again, Peace be unto you: as my Father hath sent me, even so send I you.

John 20:21

MONDAY — AUGUST 28.

O UR friend Dan saw some unusual advice when he visited the hairdresser's recently. On the wall was a humorous notice which read:

The biggest troublemaker you'll probably ever have to deal with watches you shave his face in the mirror every morning.

I later discovered that this is said to be a cowboy's proverb, a word of advice from the world of the American Wild West, but isn't it a timely reminder, too, for us all?

Many of our problems are caused, not by other people, but by ourselves!

TUESDAY — AUGUST 29.

IT had been an exciting time for Clare. She'd just moved into her first flat and, with the help of an excellent D.I.Y. manual, was busy with a host of minor repairs and improvements. When I saw her, she had just finished decorating her bedroom.

"So far, I've found most jobs quite easy," she told me. "My book comes with step-by-step diagrams. I keep thinking how nice it would be if everything in life came with such precise instructions!"

I shared her smile and yet, on reflection, I'm not sure I entirely agree. Life may not always be as smooth as a newly-plastered wall, but what an adventure it can be and, oh, the satisfaction of feeling that, despite mistakes, we have still muddled safely through!

WEDNESDAY — AUGUST 30.

COUNT your garden by the flowers,
Never by the leaves that fall.
Count your joys by golden hours,
Never when life's worries call.

Count your days by smiles, not tears,
And when birthdays come around,
Count your age by friends, not years,
And the gifts of love you've found.

THURSDAY— AUGUST 31.

I LIKE this saying, author unknown: "Success comes in cans, failure in can'ts."

September

FRIDAY — SEPTEMBER 1.

TODAY I'd like to share these thought-provoking words with you, written by the 13th-century Christian mystic Meister Eckhart, born near Erfurt in Thuringia:

"Whoever possesses God in their being, has in him a divine manner and he shines out to them in all things; for them all things taste of God and in all things it is God's image they see."

SATURDAY — SEPTEMBER 2.

ONE of my happiest childhood memories is of going to pick wild fruit such as brambles and raspberries. There was something wonderful about hunting in the hedgerows for a new treasure trove, coming home with stained fingers and full containers.

The sad truth is that we often forget just how much there is growing wild around us. It's quicker to buy a jar of jam than to go out into the lanes to hunt for the berries to make our own.

But this is one of the most exciting things we can pass on to our children and grandchildren, the joy of harvesting that Autumn crop which is waiting for us in our back roads and along our riverbanks.

SUNDAY — SEPTEMBER 3.

PRESERVE me, O God: for in thee do I put my trust.

Psalms 16:1

MONDAY — SEPTEMBER 4.

I FOUND a saying one day which was new to me. It contains so much wisdom in just a few words: "Do not forget little kindnesses, and do not remember small faults."

Perhaps we should all have these lines in front of us as we start another week. I, for one, will try to remember and act upon them.

TUESDAY — SEPTEMBER 5.

THE Lady of the House and I had spent a pleasant day pottering in the garden, making the most of the late sunshine.

"Doesn't it sometimes seem, Francis," she remarked as we were later sipping a cup of tea, "we're so busy earlier in the year it isn't until September arrives that we find time to sit down and appreciate the sunlight and the flowers."

Her words were certainly true, but they also struck me as very much like life itself. In our youth and middle years most of us are so preoccupied with all the hustle and bustle of existence that we may rarely pause to savour the world around us.

Perhaps that is why later life is sometimes described as the "golden years", for it is then that we often discover the real gold of life — the time and the wisdom to simply sit back and enjoy it all.

"CAM" DAY

WEDNESDAY — SEPTEMBER 6.

WHEN asked to name an individual who has had a remarkable life many people would nominate Ranulph Fiennes. In his life he has been knighted, has competed in seven marathons in seven days, written several books, discovered the lost city of Ubar, walked unsupported across Antarctica and been to both Poles, raising a great deal of money for charity.

But when asked which of his achievements he thought was the greatest, he didn't hesitate. Without a doubt it was his thirty-five year marriage to his wife, Victoria.

A humble and touching response from a truly gifted man.

THURSDAY — SEPTEMBER 7.

BLESSINGS FOR YOUR JOURNEY

MAY the sun spread his light on your pathway
The wind blowing warm from the west,
Your days fill with wonder and beauty,
The nights with contentment and rest.
May the blessings of hope lift your spirit
And faith always lighten your load,
The promise of happy tomorrows
Shine bright as you travel the road.
May the strength of your courage sustain you
Whenever you make a new start,
Good health and good friends never fail you
And love fill your life and your heart.

Iris Hesselden.

FRIDAY — SEPTEMBER 8.

WALKING through the market, it was with a twinge of sadness that Fred noticed the flower-stall now had bulbs for sale, for to him it always seems a sign that Summer is coming to an end.

But even as he paused in front of the counter, a customer turned to him with a smile. "I love coming to choose which bulbs to buy," she said happily. "It makes me feel as if it's almost the beginning of Spring already."

Now that's the right way to look at it!

SATURDAY — SEPTEMBER 9.

THE Lady of the House was smiling as she returned from visiting her friend. "Sandra's granddaughter Rachel was there," she told me, "and feeling rather cross and disappointed. Apparently, today was her first French lesson at school, and she'd expected to come home speaking it fluently."

My own smile was sympathetic, for there can be few of us who've never known the disappointment of not quite achieving all we thought we would. Happily, the Lady of the House had been able to come up with some cheering words from writer Louisa May Alcott:

"Far away there in the sunshine are my highest aspirations. I may not reach them but I can look up and see their beauty, believe in them, and try to follow where they lead."

Or, to put it another way for Rachel's benefit — *Courage, mon brave.* You'll get there in the end!

SUNDAY — SEPTEMBER 10.

AND one of them, when he saw that he was healed, turned back, and with a loud voice glorified God.

Luke 17:15

MONDAY— SEPTEMBER 11.

I NEVER tire of reading the witty sayings that can often be found on boards outside churches. Here's a couple:

"Searching for a new look? Have your faith lifted here!"

"No God, no peace. Know God, know peace."

TUESDAY — SEPTEMBER 12.

OUR friend Andrew is a keen handyman, so the Lady of the House couldn't resist passing on this advice to him that she came across in a magazine:

HOW TO GET ON IN LIFE

Take panes, said the window.
Never be led, said the pencil.
Do a driving business, said the hammer.
Aspire to great things, said the nutmeg grater.
Make light of everything, said the fire.
Make much of small things, said the microscope.
Never do anything off-hand, said the glove.
Just reflect, said the mirror.
Be sharp, said the knife.
Find a good thing and stick to it, said the glue.

Practical tips for everyday living for us all.

WEDNESDAY — SEPTEMBER 13.

"I'D love to do some real good in the world," sighed Stella. "It's just that the chance never seems to arise."

Hearing Stella's lament, I suspect that most of us have known that feeling. How desirable it would be, we think, to make the grand gesture that would change everything for the better. Well, it's certainly a worthwhile idea but one which, alas, can also be so seductive that we don't always notice the smaller opportunities all around us.

Next time I'm tempted to save my efforts for something important, I'll try to remember these words from the eighteenth-century German writer, Jean Paul Richter: "Do not wait for extraordinary circumstances to do good; try to use ordinary situations."

THURSDAY — SEPTEMBER 14.

OUR friends had travelled a long distance to meet us after some years spent overseas, and we exchanged greetings — a warm hug.

Just then Moira, one of our visitors, said: "Do you know, there is no such thing as a bad hug, only good ones and great ones?"

Afterwards, we thought a little about hugs, and agreed that they are welcome for a whole variety of reasons. They are fully returnable, energy efficient and appreciated in all kinds of weather.

In fact, Moira added, they are especially good for cold and rainy days and very effective in treating problems like Monday morning blues.

A hug is the ideal way to say hello or good-bye

FRIDAY — SEPTEMBER 15.

I T'S never wise to advertise
  The worries you possess.
Life's more fun if everyone
  Decides to grumble less.
Why long for things that money brings,
  Or crave for large amounts?
To gauge your worth upon this earth,
  It's what you are that counts.

John M. Robertson.

SATURDAY — SEPTEMBER 16.

THERE have been child prodigies throughout history and we might well include the youngest child of eminent preacher and hymn writer, the Rev. William Henry Havergal. From the age of seven, his daughter, Frances, was following in her father's footsteps, her verses appearing in "Good Words" and other religious periodicals.

She was of delicate health, but accompanied her father to Dusseldorf and studied there for a year. Her sympathetic nature made her an early "agony aunt", always willing to listen to the problems of others, though she found this exhausting and was heard to say: "I hope the angels will let me alone for a bit when I get to Heaven!"

How often we close our hymn book without even glancing at the author's name. Next time "Take My Life And Let It Be" or "Who Is On The Lord's Side?" is sung, spare a moment to remember the sensitive girl who wrote them, Frances Havergal (1836-79).

SUNDAY — SEPTEMBER 17.

SHEW me thy ways, O Lord; teach me thy paths.

Psalms 25:4

MONDAY — SEPTEMBER 18.

JUST the other day I overheard a leave-taking which included "Heaven attend you!"

I have always liked the French "au revoir" – goodbye for the present, with its implication of meeting again — but add the words "Heaven attend you", and you have, I think, a special farewell for those long partings which can happen in life.

TUESDAY — SEPTEMBER 19.

MANY years ago, I saw a production of a children's play. One of the main characters was named Procrastination. It's a long time ago and, I'm sorry to say, I don't remember anything else, except the children in the audience joining in, as they invariably do at a pantomime. It was great fun.

However, the word procrastination stayed with me, perhaps because I didn't know it very well in those days! The character was described as "the thief of time" and I've often thought how most of us are guilty of wasting time, which is a very special commodity.

We tend to put things off until tomorrow, next week or even next year. Perhaps we should all resolve to get on with things now and not let procrastination steal any of our precious time!

WEDNESDAY — SEPTEMBER 20.

I WAS interested to read about some research at a leading hospital. This involved a number of patients with emotional problems who had been invited to sit and listen to readings of poetry.

What effect do you think this had? Well, practically everyone said that they felt better. This result, however, would not surprise poetry-lovers who know the untold satisfaction of opening our minds to the delights of verse.

By coincidence I heard a radio presenter declare: "Poems are not just to be admired and then thrown away. They can make you laugh, change your outlook, forgive others."

If you haven't read poetry for years, make time today. You won't be disappointed.

THURSDAY — SEPTEMBER 21.

HOW young do you feel? I like to remind friends of what the writer and thinker Samuel Ullman once said:

"Whether we are sixty or sixteen, there is, in every human being's heart, the lure of wonder, the unfailing child-like appetite of what's next, and the joy of the game of living."

Ullman wanted us to visualise "a wireless station" in the centre of the heart, and to think of it as receiving messages of beauty, hope, cheer, courage and power.

"Keep your aerials up, catch the waves of optimism, and you will stay young," he said. "Years may wrinkle the skin, but to give up enthusiasm wrinkles the soul."

MELLOW
FRUITFULNESS

FRIDAY — SEPTEMBER 22.

OUR friend Davina was driving friends home from an enjoyable meeting. It was late September and the leaves were turning. The sun picked out their gold and red and there was mist on the distant hills.

Norma remarked how beautiful everything looked and Davina agreed. Then, quietly, after a few moments' thought, she added, "We're well blessed, aren't we?"

These words are worth considering. Perhaps it's easy to be optimistic on a lovely day when life is going well but it's not always so simple when things go wrong.

Sometimes, when we are feeling a little down or have a few temporary aches and pains, we should try to look around us. Be thankful for our home, our friends and the memory of happy times, reminding ourselves that we really are "well blessed".

SATURDAY — SEPTEMBER 23.

THE telephone rings, and you're feeling despondent that day . . . You're not in the mood to talk, even discuss, far less tackle a useful or important job of work. You'll know the feeling!

Our friend Peter has the answer to the situation. When this happens, he suggests, it is a good idea to "snap out of it" and remember these inspiring words:

Motivation determines what you do.
Attitude determines how well you do it.

SUNDAY — SEPTEMBER 24.

A WISE son maketh a glad father.

Proverbs 10:1

MONDAY — SEPTEMBER 25.

VISITING a friend, my eye was caught by a small toy lizard high up in a corner of the room. Seeing my bemused expression, Jan started to laugh.

"That's Larry the Lizard," she explained. "He's trying to find his way to London, but keeps getting lost!

"He's a family tradition," she went on. "When I was small my grandfather would hide him in a different place each time I visited. The first thing I always did when I came in was look for Larry. Part of me hoped he'd finally found the road to London but mostly I was relieved when he was still here, because then the fun could continue. Now I maintain this tradition for my own grandchildren and they love it as much as I did.

"I think we'll have to change his destination, though." Jan's eyes twinkled with mischief. "You see, he's already been to London. I couldn't resist taking him in my case when I went there on holiday last Summer!"

TUESDAY — SEPTEMBER 26.

TODAY I'd like to share with you these simple, but thought-provoking lines:
Sorrow looks back,
Worry looks around,
But faith looks up.

WEDNESDAY — SEPTEMBER 27.

SOMEONE is reported as having said that, with so much history behind us, every day must be the anniversary of something bad.

I prefer to look at it this way: from all that history, every day has to be the anniversary of something good and wonderful, too.

THURSDAY — SEPTEMBER 28.

AN old Nissen hut on the small Orkney island of Lamb Holm is virtually the only thing left as a reminder of Camp 60, once home to Italian prisoners during the Second World War. But what a reminder it is!

With no place of worship to call their own, the prisoners approached the camp's commander for permission to build a small chapel. He was sympathetic to their request, so the prisoners were given two Nissen huts and, using scrap metal and debris, they set to work.

Gradually, with basic materials, ingenuity and craftsmanship instead of marble, fancy tools and fine materials, the project progressed. Thousands of visitors from all over the world now visit the "Miracle of Camp 60" each year to marvel at the exquisite work of artist Domenico Chiocchetti and the band of men who built the beautiful Italian Chapel. Descendants still visit the site, too, and are welcomed to the Orkney Islands with warmth and hospitality.

Born out of the horrors of war, the beautiful Italian Chapel remains an enduring symbol of peace and friendship.

FRIDAY — SEPTEMBER 29.

NONE of us would ever want to be called a "stick-in-the-mud" — you know, the sort of person who seldom thinks of or acts on fresh ideas. We'd much prefer to be seen as people with new and bright plans, who always have contributions to make for the future.

The Chinese, thousands of years ago, encouraged innovative thoughts about their life and work, and revelled in putting them into practice. They even have a proverb which I'd like to share with you. It says: "Be not afraid of growing slowly, be afraid only of standing still."

SATURDAY — SEPTEMBER 30.

MEETING STRANGERS

YOU'RE meeting for the first time
And you feel a little shy?
You haven't found the common ground
Where mutual interests lie?
You're scared of looking silly,
Not sure what to say?
You'd almost like to turn around
And quickly walk away.
But worry not, for awkwardness
Can very soon disperse.
The other person, don't forget,
May yet be feeling worse.
So tell yourself your job it is
To help their shyness end,
And very soon I'm sure you'll find
You've made a brand-new friend.

Margaret Ingall.

October

GOD is not the God of the dead, but of the living.

Matthew 22:32

IN her book "Seasons Of My Life" Hannah Hauxwell leaned on an old iron gate and looked out over the wind-scoured Yorkshire moors around her home.

"It's my favourite place here," she said. "If I have nothing in my pocket I will always have this. It's mine for the taking and always will be . . . even when I'm no longer here."

But home for Hannah had, for decades, been an isolated farmhouse with no electricity or running water. When the last of her relatives left or died Hannah's lot was a solitary round of backbreaking work with only her animals for company, yet she loved it more than any other place.

Without question the Dales are beautiful, but I think that the true secret of Hannah's happiness lay in her faith. She knew with absolute certainty where she came from, where she belonged in this life and where she would be reunited "in the sweet bye-and-bye" with the family she loved.

TUESDAY — OCTOBER 3.

I'M sure that you've noticed how often people reveal their personalities by the way they view the world. I came across a rhyme by the American writer and librettist, Arthur Guiterman, which puts the point beautifully:

What one approves, another scorns,
And thus his nature each discloses,
You find the rose bush full of thorns,
I find the thorn bush full of roses.

I do hope you find more roses than thorns in your life!

WEDNESDAY — OCTOBER 4.

AUTUMN MORNING

AS early morning sunshine spills
Her light upon the day,
The silver mist in ghostly gown
Steals silently away.
And in the air a hint of frost —
Embroidered Autumn leaves,
And here and there pearl dewdrops glint
Amongst the barley sheaves.

Autumn makes her presence felt
In colours bright and gold,
And on nature's canvas splashes
Amber, russet, gold.
Just like a rustic tapestry
Spread out across the land,
She paints her pastoral masterpiece
Untouched by earthly hand.

Kathleen Gillum.

THURSDAY — OCTOBER 5.

WHENEVER I see the swallows gathering on the wires at the beginning of Autumn, I think of the journey ahead of them. They're about to fly all the way to Africa, these birds that weigh less than a snowball.

To me, this is visible proof of an amazing God who said: "My strength is made perfect in weakness."

FRIDAY — OCTOBER 6.

WE have come to know Great-Aunt Louisa as a wise and entertaining relative through her diaries, scrapbooks and family photographs.

Pretty and fun-loving Louisa never married, because her fiancé William, the love of her life, was killed in the Great War. Louisa was deeply unhappy for a long time afterwards. And then, sometime later, we see an entry in her diary:

"John and Martha's children loved our seaside picnic yesterday; the sun shone, we all helped to build sandcastles and we played rounders and paddled. We ate all the sandwiches, too, with just the faintest seasoning of sand! I even had a donkey ride, as did the children."

Then follows without comment these lines by George Herbert, the 17th-century poet: "Who would have thought my shrivel'd heart could have recovered greenness? It was gone quite underground."

When we suffer loss and sorrow, the passing of time does bring a measure of gentle healing; "Time brings roses", as the German proverb says.

OH, ROWAN TREE

SATURDAY — OCTOBER 7.

A FRIEND saw these memorable words in a
church magazine:
Difficult moments, seek God.
Quiet moments, worship God.
Painful moments, trust God.
Every moment, thank God.

SUNDAY — OCTOBER 8.

P RAISE the Lord with harp: sing unto him
with the psaltery and an instrument of ten
strings.

Psalms 33:2

MONDAY — OCTOBER 9.

E VER won an argument and been tempted to
be a little smug? We have all met people who
will argue black is white rather than admit they
were wrong, simply because the embarrassment of
hearing "I told you so" is more than they can
bear. And so the row might go on for ever.

I was reading about the American Civil War.
No dispute is more heartbreaking than that which
sets father against son and neighbour against
neighbour. General Grant was the most
implacable opponent the South had, but when
General Lee surrendered the Confederacy Grant
prevented his troops from cheering.

"The war is over," he declared. "The rebels are
our countrymen again."

The person you are taking issue with will
probably have been a friend or colleague before
the disagreement. A little generosity on your part
will make sure they are again.

TUESDAY — OCTOBER 10.

NEXT time the wind blows a gale, or the heavens open to unleash a rainstorm, may I suggest that you take a leaf out of the poet and writer John Ruskin's book.

Ruskin, who lived from 1819 to 1900, had a wonderful empathy with the world's changing climatic conditions, with never a bad word to say about the natural elements. An artist of renown, he would often set himself the task of painting a stormy scene at his home in Coniston in the Lake District. He loved the weather, even at its worst.

"I want you to know that sunshine is delicious, and rain is refreshing," he wrote. "The wind braces up; snow is exhilarating. There is no such thing as bad weather; we just get different kinds of good weather."

WEDNESDAY— OCTOBER 11.

PASS IT ON!

WHEN someone does you kindness
As you pass along life's way,
And it's not within your power
To return it straight away,
Then don't just shrug your shoulders
And consign it to the past,
But hang on to your feelings
And keep the memory fast.
Then when you meet another
Who needs some help from you,
Then pass it on, that kindness,
It's what you're meant to do!

Margaret Ingall.

THURSDAY — OCTOBER 12.

I OFTEN think of friendship as being like a tree. Even when Autumn comes, the leaves flutter down and a tree looks dead, the roots are still alive deep beneath the ground, strong as iron.

Often what matters most is what can't be seen, the root of love that survives all storms and will not die.

FRIDAY — OCTOBER 13.

IN 1966 a young Englishwoman named Jackie Pullinger boarded a boat and set off on a journey of faith. Too young to join a missionary society, Jackie still believed that God was telling her: "Go!" She didn't know where exactly, only that she had to obey.

She bought a ticket to take her as far as she could travel with the money she had, and when her funds ran out she got off the boat. She found herself in Hong Kong.

In the years that followed Jackie worked amongst the gang members and drug dealers of Kowloon's notorious Walled City, showing them practical love and care that helped transform hundreds of lives. The City has since been demolished, but Jackie, who was awarded the MBE, is still there, and so is the church that grew from her ministry.

Just as Jackie Pullinger had the faith to "go", despite not knowing what lay ahead, it is true that faith is believing in advance what can only be understood in reverse.

SATURDAY — OCTOBER 14.

BEN JONSON (1573-1637), the English poet and dramatist, wrote the following inspirational words:

"He knows not his own strength that hath not met adversity. Heaven prepares good men with crosses."

SUNDAY — OCTOBER 15.

AND immediately his fame spread abroad throughout all the region round about Galilee.

Mark 1:28

MONDAY — OCTOBER 16.

ONE of Europe's great thinkers, philosopher Soren Kierkegaard, loved walking around his home town of Copenhagen. In fact, he thrived on his city strolls so much that he suggested a brisk walk as a cure for all our worries and ills.

A familiar figure in the Danish capital, where he was born in 1813, he once said: "Every day I walk myself into a state of well-being and walk away from every illness. I have walked myself into my best thoughts."

Other people would readily agree with Soren's claim: "There is no thought so burdensome that you can't walk away from it."

Playwright James Barrie, of Peter Pan fame, had a saying: "Make your feet your friend," and there is a popular Irish proverb which says: "Your feet will take you where your heart is."

So why not get out your walking shoes today?

TUESDAY — OCTOBER 17.

THE Lady Of The House was enthusiastic when she told me of this "Workers' Praytime" idea she came across in a magazine. Praytime breaks are short moments when you turn your thoughts away from the demands of routine.

Here are the reflective words of one daytime prayer:

Slow me down, Lord. Ease the pounding of my heart by the quieting of my mind.

Steady my hurried pace at work, and give me, amid the confusion of my day, the calmness of the everlasting hills around us.

Teach me the art of slowing down to look at a flower, to chat with a friend, to read a few lines from a good book, or to pat a dog.

Slow me down, Lord, and inspire me as I focus for these few seconds on life's enduring values.

Words to strengthen us all today.

WEDNESDAY — OCTOBER 18.

I LIKE to think that today any one of us could suddenly have a bright idea to launch something new, exciting and useful. A project, perhaps, to improve our home? A way to help a friend overcome a problem? Or even an improvement for our village, town or city.

A busy entrepreneur called Nolan Bushnell once said: "Everyone who has ever taken a shower has an idea. But it is the person who gets out of the shower, dries off and does something about the idea, who makes a difference."

THURSDAY — OCTOBER 19.

BILL had always admired Katherine's calligraphy skills. Then she offered to teach him to write in that attractive flowing script. She asked Bill to copy a passage by Walt Whitman, the American poet:

. . . I know of nothing else but miracles . . .
To me every hour of the light and dark is a
*   miracle,*
Every cubic inch of space is a miracle,
Every square yard of the surface of the earth
*   is spread with miracles.*

"A fine sentiment," he agreed. "And all very well for a lovely Spring day or a dramatic thunderstorm but how do we get to see the boring, everyday things as miracles?"

"That's easy," Katherine replied. "Just look at them as if you had never seen them before. Then imagine how you would feel if you could never see them again."

Bill's calligraphy skills may not have improved greatly but the way he looks at the world has. And there are a lot more miracles out there than you might imagine.

FRIDAY — OCTOBER 20.

BEGIN each new day by thanking God for taking you safely through the night.

Don't start your waking hours by worrying about all you can't achieve, all the things that may be on your mind. Make a fresh beginning by thanking Him for all you do have, all that gives you reason to be glad.

SATURDAY — OCTOBER 21.

SOMEONE once asked me to do a favour for them. I hesitated before saying that I was sorry but time wouldn't allow me to lend a hand on this occasion. Saying no, especially to someone we know well, is difficult.

Most of us have become accustomed, over the years, to saying a quick and friendly yes to many invitations and requests. After all, it is so much easier than giving a negative response.

But remember, we all have a right to refuse at times and we can do so without appearing to be unkind. Just say no, as pleasantly as you can, not necessarily giving a specific reason, and the person seeking your help will understand.

Don't be in the situation of always being the person who can't say no!

SUNDAY — OCTOBER 22.

THEM that honour me I will honour, and they that despise me shall be lightly esteemed.

Samuel 1 2:30

MONDAY— OCTOBER 23.

AUTUMN sweeps around the corner,
Tossing leaves in disarray;
How they scatter in the breezes,
Never in one place to stay!
Wait until the gust's abated,
Just a lull in Autumn's day:
Rush to scoop them all together —
Oh, too late, they've blown away! . . .

Elizabeth Gozney.

TOWER OF STRENGTH

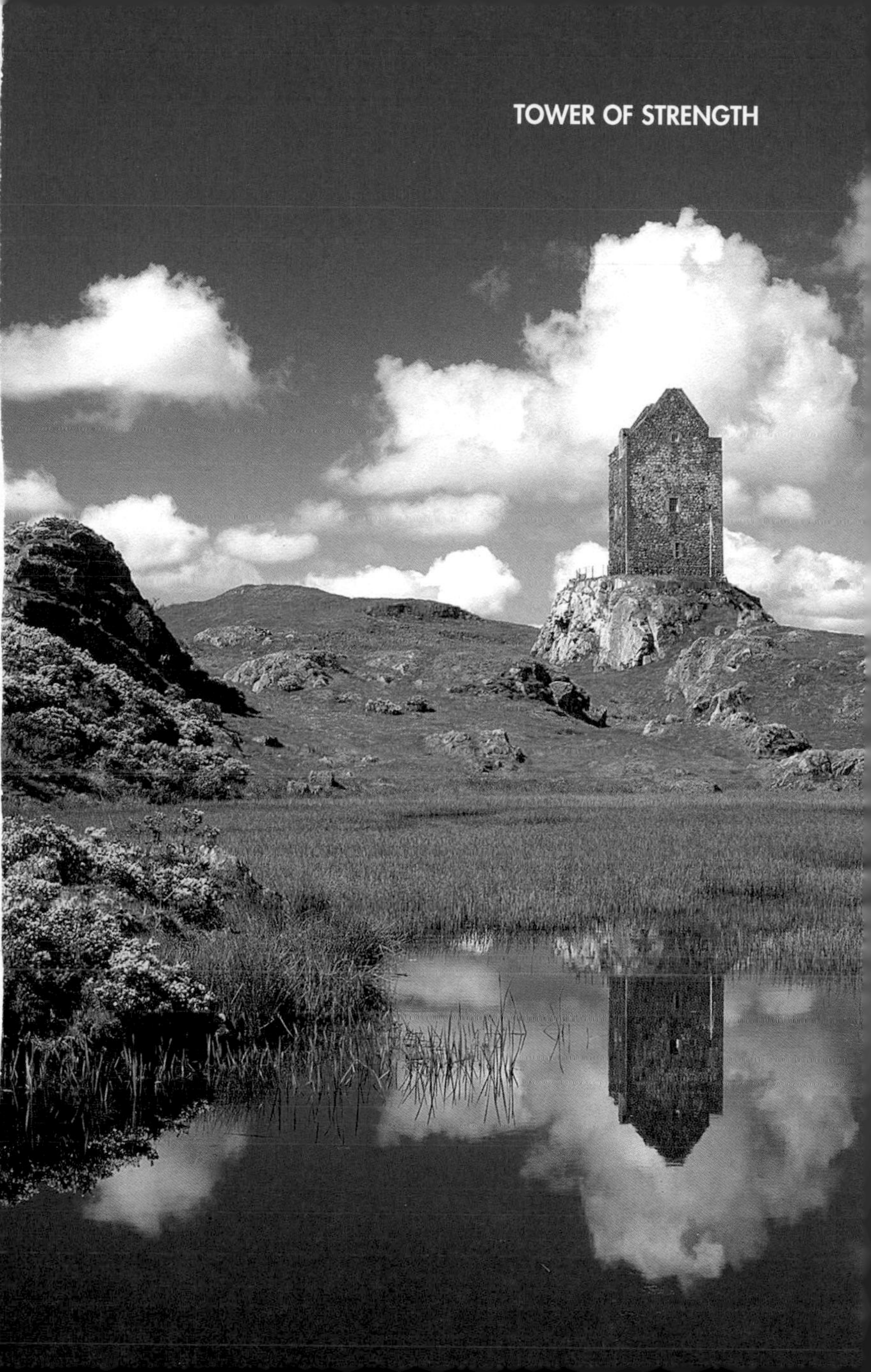

TUESDAY — OCTOBER 24.

LORRAINE, who is six years old, was being tucked up for the night when she whispered this goodnight message to her mother:

"Just put the light out, Mummy. Our teacher says not to get frightened if we see shadows in the dark because it means there must be a light shining somewhere nearby."

A thought to remember when worry and fear cast their own shades of gloom in our path.

WEDNESDAY — OCTOBER 25.

A SMALL group of friends had been meeting in their church hall for a monthly coffee morning for years, but somehow the old spark had begun to be less evident.

The hall was a little out of the way, and attendance had dropped as young mothers went back to work, people moved away or weren't able to come regularly. But the friends knew that there were lonely people in the area who would love the chance to come and meet folk for a chat.

Newer, more central premises were found and posters were put up throughout the village. Any money raised from homemade produce on sale would go to a different charity every month.

The small band of volunteers set to with enthusiasm, and gradually the word spread. Now their coffee mornings are lively affairs full of laughter and chat, looked forward to by many.

Nothing has really changed — and yet everything has changed. It reminds me of an old saying: "Preserve the old, but know the new."

THURSDAY — OCTOBER 26.

HERE is a thought that has helped many on days when things are not going too smoothly.

"Whatever the struggle, continue the climb. It may be only one step to the top."

FRIDAY — OCTOBER 27.

TODAY

YESTERDAY has gone forever —
Forget it, let it be.
Who knows what tomorrow holds?
Today's for you and me.
Another chance to start afresh
And leave the past behind,
Accomplish those unfinished tasks
And seek some peace of mind.

A time to write or make a call
Encourage someone's schemes,
And then a time for being you
To nourish all your dreams.
A time to reap, a time to sow
And every hope renew,
And celebrate this gift of life —
Today's for me and you.

Iris Hesselden.

SATURDAY — OCTOBER 28.

I ONCE caught sight of this notice in a village shop:
Remember, please, a smile is cheap,
Give one away — you get one to keep.

SUNDAY — OCTOBER 29.

AND Jesus answered them, saying, The hour is come, that the Son of man should be glorified.

John 12:23

MONDAY — OCTOBER 30.

READING about the origins of The Salvation Army I was particularly inspired by William Booth's instruction to his son. Shocked at the number of people sleeping on the streets, Booth turned to young Bramwell and said, "Go and do something."

And he did. The Salvation Army's work with homeless people has since become legendary.

Now, how many of us could "do something" like that? Well, probably more than you might think.

I don't imagine General Booth would have accepted any excuses from his son, even if he had felt like offering any. To William and Bramwell the instruction to "love thy neighbour" was present in every day of their lives.

And against these wonderful words they would hear no excuses.

TUESDAY— OCTOBER 31.

FRIENDS, books, a cheerful heart, and conscience clear,
Are the most choice companions we have here.

I thought I would share with you these words which are after my own heart, written by William Mather in 1681.

November

AT the start of the twentieth century Billy Morris was a bicycle repair boy. Thirty years later, he was Lord Nuffield, a giant in the motor industry. Having made his millions he set out to do what he had always wanted to do — good!

Hospitals and research facilities across the country and abroad benefited from his generosity and by the time he died, he had given away over thirty million pounds. An ambitious businessman and an exacting employer Lord Nuffield seems to have shown inordinate faith in his workers.

"I go on the theory," he said, "that if I've got a good man who makes a mistake that costs me half a million it would be silly to sack him. The man who replaces him might make the same mistake again, but the first fellow certainly won't."

NICHOLAS Monsarrat, author of "The Cruel Sea", knew that complicated situations could often be reduced to simple questions. If you're struggling with a decision, the following words of his might help:

"Whenever you propose to do anything, you should stop and ask yourself, 'If everyone did this, what would the world be like?' You will soon discover the right answer."

FRIDAY — NOVEMBER 3.

THE world lost a great humanitarian, internationalist and wit when Peter Ustinov died. Searching for a few words to sum him up is an impossible task. He had views on virtually every subject and they were almost always charitable and kind, with a good amount of humour included.

Knowing that no marriage lasts without overcoming a series of hurdles I was drawn to his take on the subject.

"Love," he said, "is an act of endless forgiveness, a tender look which becomes a habit."

SATURDAY — NOVEMBER 4.

WHEN our friend Beatrice celebrated her birthday, one of her best friends phoned to serenade her with a rendition of the song "Happy Birthday To You".

Later she learned that this song, written in 1893 by two sisters in Kentucky, is the world's best-known one and is sung more times than any other. In fact, with each one of us having a birthday every twelve months, it is obvious that its happy and friendly words are being sung and heard somewhere every minute of every day.

Mildred and Patty Hill, its authors, first wrote the song as "Good Morning To You". Then, in 1935, a far-seeing song publisher decided to give it a makeover.

I'm sure we all know someone with a birthday to celebrate, if not today, then maybe next week.

SUNDAY — NOVEMBER 5.

THE Lord be between me and thee, and between my seed and thy seed for ever.

Samuel 1, 20: 42

MONDAY — NOVEMBER 6.

I WAS leafing through a book of treasured quotations when I found this saying, and I'd like to pass it on:

"Blessed is the individual who is so busy that he has no time to worry in the daytime, and has kept himself so occupied that he finds himself too sleepy to worry at night."

TUESDAY — NOVEMBER 7.

EVEN though the sun's not shining
And the sky is dull and grey,
Even though you watched the postman
Walk straight past your door today.
Even though the phone's not ringing
When you wished and hoped it would,
Look around you, count your blessings,
Life is precious, life is good.

Even when you're disappointed
And your plans have gone awry,
Even when the friends you trusted
Never call, or walk on by.
Put these troubled thoughts behind you,
Look ahead, the way you should,
Tell yourself, with each new morning,
Life is precious, life is good!

Iris Hesselden.

THE FALL

WEDNESDAY — NOVEMBER 8.

"GOOD old Duncan," remarked the Lady of the House, as we said goodbye to a friend after hearing all about his disastrous attempts at some D.I.Y. plumbing. "He always reminds me of a tea-kettle."

"A tea-kettle?" I enquired, somewhat startled.

"Well, you know the old saying," she reminded me. "Optimism is the cheerful frame of mind that enables a tea-kettle to sing, even though in hot water up to its nose."

I laughed, for it certainly summed up Duncan. The next time I find myself struggling with a task, I'll do my best to keep whistling!

THURSDAY — NOVEMBER 9.

I MUST admit I'd never heard of John Burroughs until I went to a talk at a local village hall, but I soon learned what a fascinating life he had led. Born in the beautiful Catskill Mountains in 1817, he grew up with a keen love of nature, and was a pioneer in conservation long before most people recognised its importance.

One of the things he wrote struck a particular chord with me: "To find the universal elements enough; to find the air and water exhilarating; to be refreshed by a morning walk or an evening saunter; to be thrilled by the stars at night; to be elated over a bird's nest or a wildflower in Spring — these are some of the rewards of a simple life."

Now that was a man who really got his priorities right.

FRIDAY — NOVEMBER 10.

WHO decides what kind of day you have? Why, you do, of course! No matter what the day brings, it's how you handle it that matters. Sometimes, though, as this anonymous poem says, we could all do with a little help:

So far today I've done all right.
I haven't gossiped, lost my temper,
Been greedy or grumpy,
Been nasty or selfish.
I'm very thankful for that . . .
But in a few minutes, God,
I'm going to get out of bed
And from then on I'll probably need
A lot more help.

SATURDAY — NOVEMBER 11.

"BEAUTY," as the saying goes, "is in the eye of the beholder," and I agree. We all have our preferences as to what makes life especially enjoyable, and they include many different things.

Whether we define "beautiful" as the sight of a wonderful view, the sound of the sea or a symphony, the fragrance of a Summer's evening, or even (as has been pronounced by a friend!) the taste of the Lady of the House's coffee cake, the list is endless.

"Anyone," said Kafka, "who keeps the ability to see beauty never grows old."

I certainly like to think that's true — and aren't we lucky to have so many different kinds to choose from?

SUNDAY — NOVEMBER 12.

THE earth is the Lord's, and the fulness thereof; the world, and they that dwell therein.

Psalms 24: 1

MONDAY — NOVEMBER 13.

AFTER I read these words from the Dalai Lama I stopped to read them again, convinced at first that I had either misread or there had been a misprint.

"If you want others to be happy," he said, "practise compassion. If you want to be happy, practise compassion."

It's simple, it's straightforward . . . and it's absolutely true.

TUESDAY — NOVEMBER 14.

IT is wise never to dismiss the small things in life. Like, for instance, the gentle drip-drip of a raindrop. As the verse says:

One little unshed raindrop
May think itself too small,
Yet somewhere a thirsty flower
Awaits its fall.

Equally, all that we say to each other in everyday conversation may appear as nothing in particular at the time but:

One little word unspoken,
May seem too small to say,
But somewhere for that one word
A heart may pray.

These thoughts on all things small are from the poet Helen Thomas Allison.

WEDNESDAY — NOVEMBER 15.

THE clergyman was trying to compose his Sunday sermon. Outside his study window Jeremy, his teenage son, was working on his recently acquired motor bike.

To the undiscerning eye, it looked like a heap of rusty machinery. Though it had taken most of Jeremy's holiday earnings and now required all of his spare time to get into a roadworthy condition, it was his life-long dream come true.

His father was irritated by constant revving up, hammering and tinkering. It was hard enough to concentrate on his demanding task when silence reigned, but with that noise it was truly impossible.

He threw down his pen and opened the window, about to make a crisp comment when he heard Jeremy say to an admiring neighbour, "Any time you want to borrow my bike, just take it."

Quietly, he closed the window. He had his text: "The Lord loveth a cheerful giver."

THURSDAY — NOVEMBER 16.

LYDIA is a great believer in the theory that the best classroom in the world is "at the feet of an elderly person".

She reminded me one day of what the writer Charles Marowitz claimed: "Old age is like climbing a mountain. The higher you get to the top, the more extensive your view becomes, and the more clearly you see the world below. You see right above the differences that divide people, and well beyond the petty hurts that annoy."

MOTHER'S PRIDE

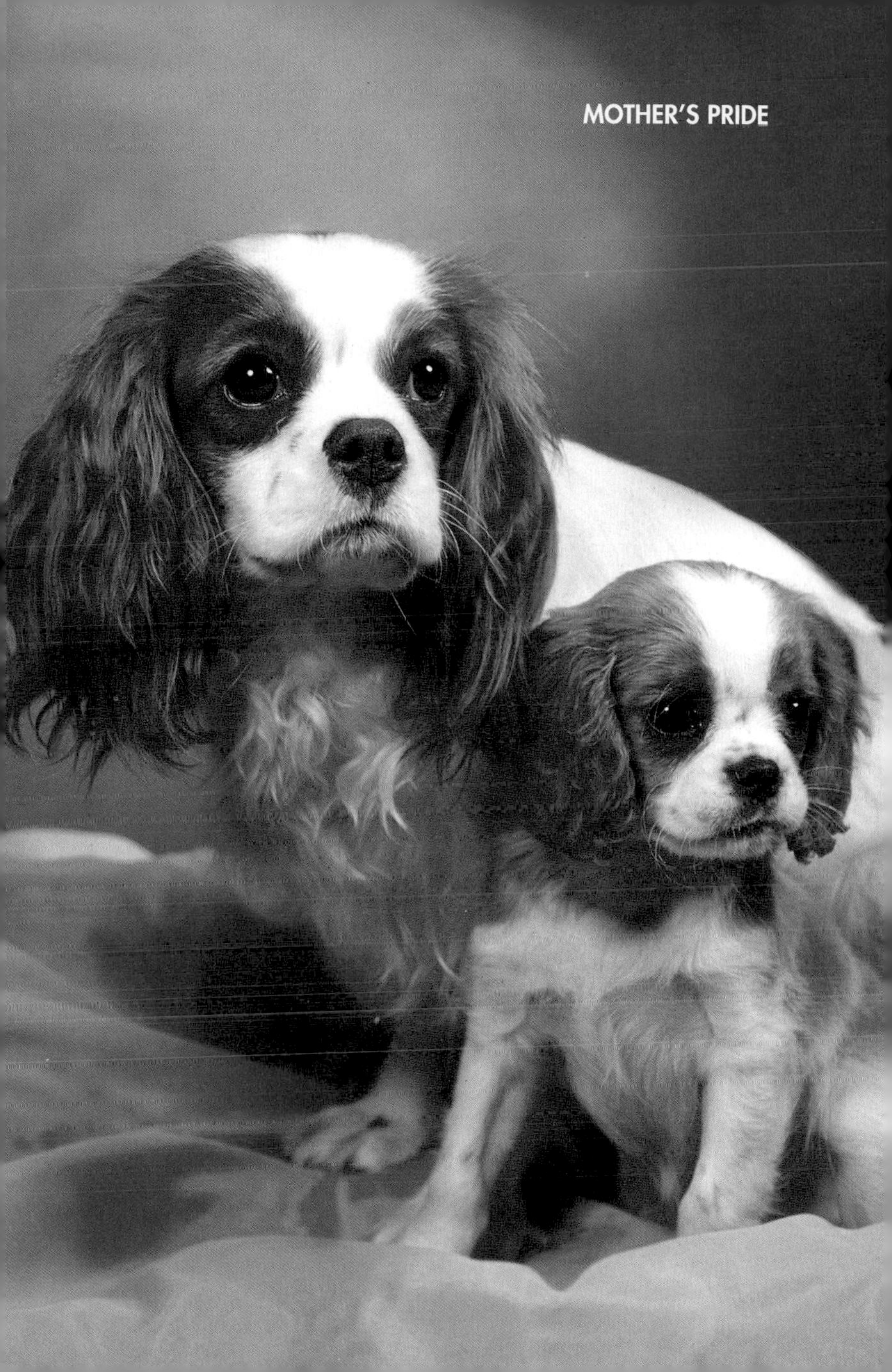

FRIDAY — NOVEMBER 17.

WHEN Marion and her friend Dora first fell out, neither imagined the breach would be serious. However, as the weeks and months passed with both insisting that the other was to blame, it began to seem as if things might never be put right.

Fortunately, a village celebration made both realise how foolish they were being and, with hugs and apologies, they resolved to put the matter behind them.

Marion and Dora are once more enjoying each other's friendship, and indeed are soon to share a holiday.

"Forgiveness does not change the past, but it does enlarge the future," Paul Boese wrote.

Marion and Dora would be first to agree!

SATURDAY — NOVEMBER 18.

PHYLLIS Bentley became one of Yorkshire's most popular novelists, but few knew how hard it had been for her in her early years. Her father owned a textile mill in Halifax and neither he nor her mother took Phyllis' writing ambitions seriously.

They expected her, as their unmarried daughter, to devote herself to domestic duties. For years she nursed her mother who had become a chronic invalid.

It says much for Phyllis' determination that when she died aged eighty-two she had written nearly thirty novels and won the love of a host of admirers.

SUNDAY — NOVEMBER 19.

WHILE the earth remaineth, seedtime and harvest, and cold and heat, and summer and winter, and day and night shall not cease.

Genesis 8:22

MONDAY — NOVEMBER 20.

DEAR Lord, you know this day has been
Not perfect, I confess.
My fault, it's true, yet still I ask
Your pardon, nonetheless.
I didn't wake rejoicing
In your sky of perfect blue,
But kept my mind fixed grimly on
The jobs I had to do.
I didn't thank you for the friends
Who called to give support,
And even when my work was done,
To you I gave no thought.
But now, dear Lord, as evening falls
And light and darkness meld,
I offer up this day to you,
With thanks for all it held.

Margaret Ingall.

TUESDAY — NOVEMBER 21.

DO you love your neighbour? It isn't always easy. That great writer, C. S. Lewis, was aware of the difficulties and he said this:

"Do not waste time bothering about whether you love your neighbour. Act as if you did . . . When you are behaving as if you love someone, you will presently come to love him."

WEDNESDAY — NOVEMBER 22.

WHEN Reginald Heber wrote "Palestine", which went on to win the Newdigate Prize for poetry at Brasenose College, Oxford, the writer Walter Scott commented that there was no reference to the temple having been built without tools. It didn't take Heber long to add:

No hammer fell, no ponderous axes rung;
Like some tall palm the mystic fabric sprung.
Majestic silence!

It was an early indication of a gift for words which later produced the well-loved "Brightest And Best Of The Sons Of The Morning", "Holy, Holy, Holy" and "From Greenland's Icy Mountains". He took orders in 1807 and, as Rev. Reginald Heber, was eventually persuaded to become Bishop of Calcutta, a charge which included the whole of British India. Those who knew him said he was wise, energetic, tactful and lovable, but in three short years the burden proved to be too great and he died.

No doubt he left quite a library, but it was unlikely to match that of his brother Richard, a noted bibliophile, whose collection ran to a total of 146,827 volumes.

THURSDAY — NOVEMBER 23.

WE plan for each tomorrow
For the joys upon the way;
But let us still remember
The joys we have today!

Elizabeth Gozney.

FRIDAY — NOVEMBER 24.

CHOOSING the right present for the right person can be difficult. But for gifts that benefit the giver as much as the recipient, why not follow Francis Maitland Balfour's advice? He suggested the following:

"To your enemy, give forgiveness; to an opponent, tolerance; to a friend, your heart; to your child, a good example; to a father, deference; to your mother, conduct that will make her proud of you; to yourself, respect; to all men, charity."

SATURDAY — NOVEMBER 25.

WHEN reading a book about Christian customs and festivals, I came across one which was new to me and, perhaps, to you. It's the Sunday before Advent, "Stir-Up Sunday".

It seems that traditionally, Christmas pudding was made then, each family member stirring the mixture for good luck. A prayer for this day adds to the meaning behind the name. It begins with the words: "Stir up, we beseech Thee, O Lord, the will of Thy faithful people."

Wouldn't it be wonderful if there could be a "Stir-Up Sunday" at regular intervals throughout the year? Sometimes we lose focus both in our lives and in our worship.

SUNDAY — NOVEMBER 26.

LET the words of my mouth, and the meditation of my heart, be acceptable in thy sight, O Lord, my strength and my redeemer.

Psalms 19:14

MONDAY — NOVEMBER 27.

I WONDER if you know these words — "make good things from ill things best from worst"?

Surely inspiring words to follow. They were written by the poet Elizabeth Barrett Browning.

The story of her life is a fascinating one. Born into a wealthy family in 1806, much of her life was spent as an invalid. Although encouraged by her father to write poetry and plays, Elizabeth's family life in London was not a happy one.

Later, in spite of her father's opposition, she eloped with and married the poet Robert Browning in 1846 and went to live in Italy.

Their marriage was one of mutual love and support, and Elizabeth had a son when she was forty-three. Robert's pet name for her was "The Portuguese", because of her colouring. Her famous "Sonnets From The Portuguese" contain these lines:

"I love thee to the level of every day's most quiet need, by sun and candlelight, I love thee freely . . ."

Elizabeth died in Italy aged fifty-five. After her death her husband prepared her last poems for publication, a true labour of love.

TUESDAY — NOVEMBER 28.

ARE you looking for something useful to do today? Here's an idea I came across when I read these words on a bulletin board:

No one can help everybody, but everybody can help somebody.

It's a thought well worth acting upon!

WEDNESDAY — NOVEMBER 29.

A MUCH-ACCLAIMED preacher was invited to a new church. He delivered his rousing sermon without shouting or raising his voice.

Afterwards someone asked, "How can a quiet man like that be such a great evangelist?"

The reply came: "It is true that he does not roar like a foghorn. He has a better way — he shines like a lighthouse."

THURSDAY — NOVEMBER 30.

SOME friends and I were discussing how we should all be more satisfied with what we have and who we are. Not always easy, I know, but then I found this Chinese tale which illustrates what we had in mind!

A lowly stonecutter was unhappy with his lot and wished to be a wealthy merchant. His wish was granted, but he was dissatisfied, so then wished to be a high official carried in a sedan chair. Again he got his wish, but he was still unhappy.

Then, in turn, he wished to be the sun, so powerful, and then a cloud to hide the sun, and then the wind to blow away the cloud. But then the wind encountered something too strong to be moved: a very large stone. The man wished to be that immovable stone.

In the silence the stone recognised the sound of hammer and chisel and knew that far below worked a lowly stonecutter.

This story doesn't tell us if he learned a lesson, but it's worth thinking about, isn't it?

December

GOOD friends and neighbours were a godsend to Robert Louis Stevenson, the author of well-loved classic novels such as "Treasure Island" and "Kidnapped".

Despite poor health, he wrote thousands of words each day in a prolific output of poems, essays and novels. His poetry captured the joy of childhood and this is my favourite quotation from an author who loved friendship and nature:

"The best things in life are those that are nearest to you: light in your eyes, flowers at your feet, duties at your hand, the path of right just before you.

"Do not grasp at the stars, but do life's plain, common work as it comes, certain that daily duties and daily bread are the sweetest things in life".

HERE'S a thought-provoking Scottish saying by a Rev. Houston, from a book entitled "Prayers And Graces":

"Lord, Thou'rt like a wee moosie peepin' oot of a hole in the wall, for Thou see'st us, but we canna see Thee."

PEAK OF
PERFECTION

THE FRIENDSHIP BOOK

SUNDAY — DECEMBER 3.

VERILY, verily, I say unto you, If a man keep my saying, he shall never see death.

John 8:51

MONDAY — DECEMBER 4.

THESE thoughtful lines are taken from a poem by Japanese poet, Mitsuo Aida:

Because there are employees,
There can be company presidents;
Because there are juniors,
There can be seniors;
Because there are students,
There can be teachers.

Because there are people who buy,
Things can be sold;
Because there are people who sell,
Things can be bought.
And because there are people
Who read my clumsy work,
I can become a writer.

TUESDAY — DECEMBER 5.

LET me share with you today these words of the great French writer Victor Hugo, author of "Les Miserables". Poet, novelist and playwright, Hugo was born in 1802 in Besançon and died in Paris in 1885.

"Certain thoughts are prayers. There are moments when whatever be the attitude of the body, the soul is on its knees."

I'm sure very few of us would deny the truth of these words.

WEDNESDAY — DECEMBER 6.

CORRIE ten Boom was, perhaps, an unexpected heroine and role model. Born in Amsterdam in 1892 into a loving family, she followed in her father's footsteps and trained as a watchmaker. In 1922 she became the first female licensed watchmaker in the Netherlands.

She was 48 years old when the Nazis invaded and her life was changed forever. Her family risked everything to hide those seeking sanctuary.

Eventually, in 1944 Corrie ended up in the notorious prison camp Ravensbruck. She was released in 1945 and for the rest of her long life Corrie was a "Tramp For The Lord" — the title of one of her many books.

Travelling the world as an itinerant preacher, she obediently went wherever she felt God was telling her to go. Often she had no money, no means of travel, and nowhere to stay.

She explained her chosen life in these simple words: "Never be afraid to trust an unknown future to a known God."

THURSDAY — DECEMBER 7.

TWO and a half thousand years ago, the Chinese philosopher Confucius wrote these words which are still relevant to us today.

"To put the world in order, we must first put the nation in order; to put the nation in order, we must put the family in order; to put the family in order, we must cultivate our personal life; and to cultivate our personal life, we must first set our hearts right."

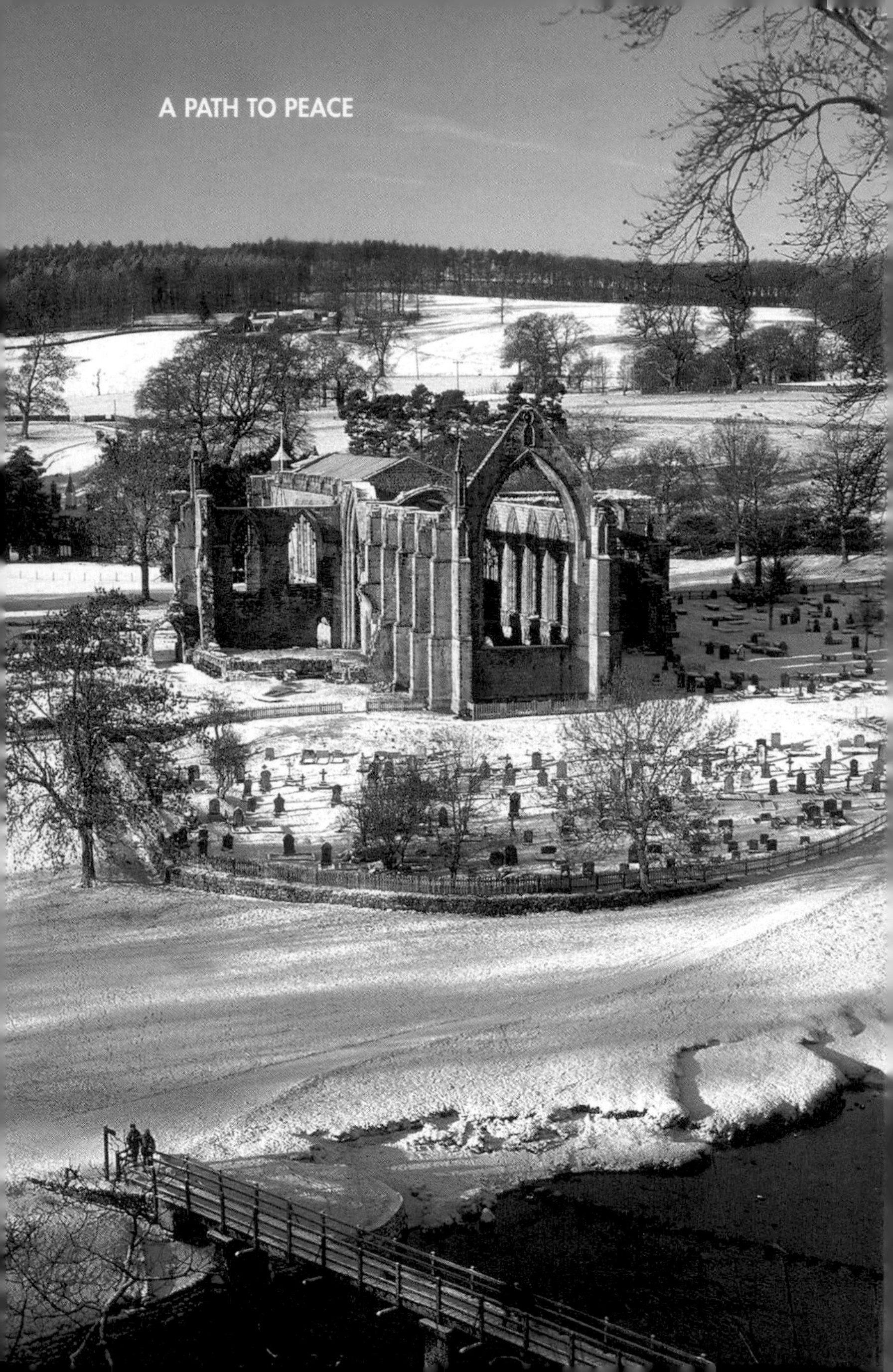
A PATH TO PEACE

FRIDAY — DECEMBER 8.

ANNIE Johnson Flint was born in New Jersey in 1866 and her life was far from easy. She and her sister lost their mother in childhood and her father's new wife didn't take to them. Annie trained to be a teacher but increasingly painful arthritis meant she had to leave teaching after only two years but she wrote these encouraging words, despite her setbacks:

God hath not promised skies always blue,
Flower-strewn pathways all our lives through.
God hath not promised sun without rain,
Joy without sorrow, peace without pain.
But God hath promised strength for the day,
Rest for the labour, light for the way,
Grace for the trials, help from above,
Unfailing sympathy, undying love.

SATURDAY — DECEMBER 9.

JOHN, a businessman friend, gives much thought to ways of making life happy for his loyal staff and productive for the customers who purchase his products.

I was discussing with him one day the various methods, old as well as new, which bring the best and happiest results at work, as well as at home.

"You know, Francis," he said, "one of the finest rules to set yourself is always to be full of optimism, and to forge ahead when others are crying failure."

John then produced a card bearing these words of Winston Churchill: *Attitude is a little thing that makes a big difference.*

SUNDAY — DECEMBER 10.

O GIVE thanks unto the Lord; for he is good; for his mercy endureth for ever.

Chronicles I 16:34

MONDAY — DECEMBER 11.

O NE day, the postman brought a welcome delivery to the door — a letter from our friend Joan, who stays in the south of France. We love receiving her news, and the Lady of the House echoed my own thoughts as she observed that even in these days of instant online communication, there is still nothing quite like an old-fashioned letter for bringing people together.

American writer Phyllis Theroux once summed it up beautifully: "To send a letter is a good way to go somewhere without moving anything but your heart."

TUESDAY — DECEMBER 12.

I N all the rush and excitement of preparing for Christmas it is easy to forget that for many people it can be a difficult time, especially for those who have lost loved ones.

One of our local churches has thought of an unusual idea. During Advent people are invited to write names of those they have lost on a candle-shaped card and hang it on a large "Lights Of Life" Christmas tree which stands in a lighted window.

Beside the tree is the text:
Blessed are those who mourn,
For they shall be comforted.

WEDNESDAY — DECEMBER 13.

SPORTING legend Jesse Owens' success started as a schoolboy, when he broke world record after world record at junior level. He reached the pinnacle of his career at the 1936 Olympic Games, when he won four gold medals.

However, this was only a small part of a life that was devoted to helping others. An inspirational speaker, he travelled widely, addressing groups all over the world. A great deal of his time was spent working with under-privileged youth.

Jesse Owens won medals, was given awards, had streets named after him, and was presented with the highest honour, the Medal of Freedom. But through it all he never lost sight of the things that matter most in life. As he said, "Awards become corroded, friends gather no dust."

THURSDAY — DECEMBER 14.

IT'S always a pleasure when the Lady of the House and I are invited to attend events held at our local primary school, and we never cease to admire the way in which Kathleen, the head teacher, has created such a happy place of learning.

Over many years she has guided both the children and her younger colleagues with great kindness and wisdom. In fact, Kathleen reminds me of these words from Samuel Taylor Coleridge:

"Advice is like snow; the softer it falls, the longer it dwells upon, and the deeper it sinks into, the mind."

That's a thought which isn't cold comfort.

FRIDAY — DECEMBER 15.

WE can all, at times, get wrapped up in our own worries but these beautiful words, left to us by Anne Frank, certainly help set things in their proper perspective:

"The best remedy for those who are afraid, lonely, or unhappy is to go outside, somewhere where they can be quite alone with the heavens, nature, and God.

"Because only then does one feel that all is as it should be and that God wishes to see people happy amidst the simple beauty of nature."

SATURDAY — DECEMBER 16.

OUR old friend Mary was privileged to attend a talk just before Christmas on the subject of simplicity. The speaker that evening had chosen the word carefully and it set everyone thinking.

"Christmas," she told her audience, "should be simple, but we can make it complicated. Indeed our lives should be simple, but we tend to make them ever more complicated."

This is often true. Just think about it for a moment. After all, we rush around buying things we sometimes don't really need and how many times have we made elaborate, stress-filled arrangements? The speaker's message was — slow down.

Let's try to have fewer unnecessary complications in our daily lives. Perhaps, by 25th December, we will have learned how to keep things just a little simpler.

SUNDAY — DECEMBER 17.

AND thou, child, shalt be called the prophet of the Highest: for thou shalt go before the face of the Lord to prepare his ways.

Luke 1:76

MONDAY — DECEMBER 18.

GREETINGS and meetings
  Are so much a part,
Of the Christmas tradition
  So dear to each heart;
And thoughts full of kindness
  Soon spread far and wide,
Enhancing the meaning
  Of true Christmastide . . .

Elizabeth Gozney.

TUESDAY — DECEMBER 19.

YOU know, I always feel there's something about this time of year that defies all definition. Christmas can be such a plum-pudding mixture of anticipation and reflection that should a passing visitor from outer space ever happen to ask questions most of us would be hard pressed to explain all the things that this season can encompass.

Yet writer Agnes M. Pharo makes a good attempt. "What is Christmas?" she pondered. "It is tenderness for the past, courage for the present, hope for the future. It is a fervent wish that every cup may overflow with blessings rich and eternal, and that every path may lead to peace."

WEDNESDAY — DECEMBER 20.

I HAVE a collection of books to inspire me with morning and evening prayers. Some are very old and have been in our family for generations, but others are modern and full of chatty, flowing thoughts.

I read of an interview with Mother Teresa of Calcutta. "What do you say to God when you pray?" Dan Rather asked her.

Mother Teresa just looked at him and then she said quietly, "I listen." Not to be daunted, he tried again. "Well, then, what does God say?"

Mother Teresa smiled. "He listens."

THURSDAY — DECEMBER 21.

CHARLES Dickens, the famous Victorian novelist, wanted people to celebrate Christmas all year round, not just in December. The heartwarming days on both sides of 25th December meant much to the man who created Ebenezer Scrooge, the selfish, Christmas-hating miser.

Great Britain, during the Industrial Revolution of the 1800s, was a land where the wealthy lived in luxury yet many were very poor. Dickens remained a passionate advocate of optimism in the face of despair.

"There is always something in life to be thankful for," he said. "I will honour Christmas in my heart and try to keep it all year round. It transforms us. This is the season of merry Christmases, friendships, cheerful recollections and affection. God bless every Christmas!"

FRIDAY — DECEMBER 22.

A SMILE is a window on your face to show that your heart is at home.

SATURDAY — DECEMBER 23.

NOT long ago I read these words: "To perceive Christmas through its wrapping becomes more difficult with every year".

E. B. White.

But not, I think, in Sarah's case. A table in her sitting-room is always piled high with an assortment of cheerful wrapping paper, coloured tissue paper, little boxes and bows and many spools of sparkling parcel ribbon.

Sarah has often said, "It gives me great pleasure to choose small gifts, nothing grand, just reminders to let friends and family know that I am thinking of them. I have always believed that part of a gift is its presentation, so I try to wrap my presents to give pleasure by the way they look."

Sarah's talents are much in demand at charity fund-raising events, when she will happily wrap presents for a small donation.

I think we can all perceive Christmas through Sarah's wrapping!

SUNDAY — DECEMBER 24.

AND the angel said unto them, Fear not: for, behold, I bring you good tidings of great joy, which shall be to all people.

Luke 2:10

MONDAY — DECEMBER 25.

A PRAYER AT CHRISTMAS

THE shepherds heard the Angel's news,
  The Wise Men travelled far,
And there was wonder, joy and hope
  For all who saw the star.

Now, Father, once more help us seek
  The joy of Christmas night,
And spread the news across the earth
  Of endless life and light.

And, Father, may we share Your love
  In heart and soul and mind,
And send Your blessings round the world
  With peace for all mankind.

Iris Hesselden.

TUESDAY — DECEMBER 26.

THE Lady of the House and I know and love a certain pretty, sheltered garden by the sea, where the evergreen, blue-flowered, aromatic rosemary — *ros marinus,* dew of the sea — thrives, and happily seeds itself.

Unlike the holly and the ivy, rosemary is perhaps not immediately associated by many of us with Christmas, and yet there is an old and lovely seasonal tradition which says that in some places rosemary will flower at midnight on Old Christmas Eve, a sign of holiness it shares with the Glastonbury Thorn.

Rosemary for remembrance of the birth of Christ.

UNSEEN
HAND

WEDNESDAY — DECEMBER 27.

MOLLY was more than a bit fed up. She'd been to consult her doctor and had been told that her vocal cords needed complete rest. In fact, she wasn't to speak a single word for six months!

How could she cope with a husband and four children if she wasn't able to talk to them? Still, she'd have to give it a go somehow, she knew.

When she needed to communicate with one of her children, she blew a whistle to attract their attention. Any instructions she wrote on slips of paper. Answers to questions were also written.

Eventually, the six months passed, and Molly reflected on her experience: "I don't think I'll ever overstretch my voice like I used to," she remarked.

As for the notes she scribbled, she admitted: "You'd be surprised how many, hastily written, I crumpled up and threw into the bin before anyone could see them. Seeing my words written down made me realise how often we speak before thinking."

Maybe we should all take a leaf out of Molly's notepad.

THURSDAY — DECEMBER 28.

SOME people believe time can work wonders. You're feeling low? "Just give it time." You've suffered sadness? "In time you'll forget."

I remember what a wise old minister once told me, "Yes, time heals many wounds, but love heals them all."

FRIDAY — DECEMBER 29.

A LITTLE country church not far away is many centuries old. The Lady of the House and I walked past it one afternoon and saw this modern-sounding notice on the door:

Think Metric —
Observe the Ten Commandments.

SATURDAY — DECEMBER 30.

I MUST confess I don't know much about baseball. Terms like hot corner, bullpen, fork ball and double steal don't mean much to me. Arch Ward, on the other hand, would have been well acquainted with all those expressions. A well-known promoter and sports editor, he was steeped in the game.

However, Arch's talents weren't confined to baseball, as this verse shows. As we celebrate one year drawing to a close, and look to a new one ahead, his simple words can be understood and enjoyed by us all:

The book is closed, the year is done,
The pages full of tasks begun.
A little joy, a little care,
Along with dreams, are written there.
This new day brings another year,
Renewing hope, dispelling fear.
And we may find before the end,
A deep content, another friend.

SUNDAY — DECEMBER 31.

THE grace of our Lord Jesus Christ be with you.   Corinthians I 16:23

The Photographs

SERENITY — *Iona Abbey.*
CLIMB EVERY MOUNTAIN — *On Ben Cleuch, Ochil Hills.*
HERALDS OF SPRING — *Borough Beck, Helmsley, North Yorkshire.*
WATER FEATURE — *Carlingwark Loch, Castle Douglas.*
THE GUARDIAN — *Corbiere Lighthouse, Jersey.*
A GOLDEN MOMENT — *Edinburgh Castle.*
ALL TOGETHER NOW! — *Lower Slaughter, Gloucestershire.*
ALMOST THERE — *Scarborough.*
TRANQUIL WATERS — *Symonds Yat, Herefordshire.*
HIGHLAND HOME — *Crathes Castle, Banchory.*
GREEN, GREEN GRASS OF HOME — *View over Crow Trees,*
near Muker, Swaledale.
"CAM" DAY — *Bridge Of Sighs, St John's College, Cambridge.*
OH, ROWAN TREE — *On the slopes of Ben A'an, the Trossachs.*
TOWER OF STRENGTH — *Smailholm Tower, near Kelso.*
THE FALL — *Swan Green, New Forest.*
PEAK OF PERFECTION — *Bla Bheinn, Isle of Skye.*
A PATH TO PEACE — *Bolton Abbey, Wharfedale.*
UNSEEN HAND — *Looking out from Fingal's Cave, Staffa.*

ACKNOWLEDGEMENTS: **Matt Bain;** In The Pink. **David Bigwood;** Pulling Her Weight, Pageboy. **James D. Cameron;** Oh, Rowan Tree. **David Gowans;** Braving The Cold. **V. K. Guy**; Catwalk, The Guardian, A Golden Moment, Best Friends, Tranquil Waters, The Fall, Mother's Pride. **Dennis Hardley;** "Cam" Day. **C. R. Kilvington;** Deep Roots, All Together Now!, Almost There, Green, Green Grass Of Home, A Path To Peace. **Duncan I. McEwan;** Tower Of Strength. **Oakleaf;** Highland Home, Mellow Fruitfulness. **Willie Shand;** Ice House, Climb Every Mountain, Under Summer Skies, Fun Of The Fair, Peak Of Perfection, Unseen Hand. **Sheila Taylor;** Serenity. **SW Images**; Water Feature. **Richard Watson;** Heralds Of Spring.

Printed and Published by D. C. Thomson & Co., Ltd.,
185 Fleet Street, London EC4A 2HS.
ISBN 1-84535-050-2